MW01624313

The Awakened Soul

Published by Lisa Hagan Books
Bracey, Virginia

Cover and Interior Design by Inna Savchuk

ISBN: 978-1-945962-38-7
Printed in U.S.A

Dear Heidi,

THE AWAKENED SOUL

May the light from your eyes

Discovering the Light Within

a spiritual memoir

continue to shine. You are a gift.

Love Lynn xoxo

LYNN PATNER, M.S.W.

LISA HAGAN BOOKS

"Love the fact that your book is shining a light on how everyone has a core wound of not being enough and I want to thank you for your invaluable contribution." **—Jack Canfield, Author of *Chicken Soup for the Soul***

In Patner's debut book, ***The Awakened Soul*** *she shares funny and moving stories of how she found her own form mysticism, how she learned to heal herself and show clients how to do the same. We learn how our mindsets are shaped and programmed by our earliest years of life and serve as our personal life compass. In order to affect meaningful changes in our life, we must learn and become aware of our unconscious programming to step into the life we desire.*

By stepping out onto your path of enlightenment, your journey will be supported ten-fold in surprising and exciting ways.

The journey goes by faster and easier if we let go of our perceived control over the outcome and allow our Guides to assist us. All one has to do is say, I am ready to step into the world of discovering who I am and why I was born.

The world is waiting for you all to remember who you are. Let go, set your intention to be the Light Being that you are. As you heal yourself, you heal the world with your love. So be it.

"Lynn Patner has nailed it. This is how you do the inward journey of self-awareness using simple, easy-to-use methods taught by the mystics. A poignant memoir of self-discovery that will inspire you to dive into your own spiritual journey of discovery and empowerment." **—Atherton Drenth, Author of *The Intuitive Dance***

"In Patner's captivating debut she interweaves stories with guidance on how you can discover your life's purpose and let your brilliant light shine." **—Betsy Chasse, Co-Writer, Director and Producer of the hit film *What The Bleep Do We Know?!.***

"In ***The Awakened Soul****, we learn how our minds and self-concepts are formed throughout our childhood and, we learn how we can free ourselves of unconscious thought patterns that may block us from becoming the person we are truly meant to be—living the life we'd most like to live."* **—Elaine Clayton, Author of *The Way of the Empath***

DEDICATION

To Michael, Rana, Andy,
Gregg and Maria.

And to my three dividends,
Noah, Mikaela and Deven.

Whose love and belief in
me have been my greatest
support along this journey.

And to Aaron and my
Team of Beings who pushed,
prodded and supported
with love my soul's message
and assist me in birthing it.

INTRODUCTION

Many people have wondered what their life's purpose is. The concept of a life purpose seems grandiose, a calling of some kind, a challenge of substantive proportions.

What does a life purpose even entail?

A desire to know why we were born. But how do we know why we were born? Can we ask ourselves such a question? Previously, I had never even thought about it.

Why would anyone want to embark on such a deeply personal, philosophical, and mystical journey?

Personally, I did not.

I had absolutely no desire to know on a cellular level why I was born. But thirty-six years ago, I did not have a choice, as my soul had a blueprint meticulously carved out for me, and it was the furthest from anything I could have ever imagined. I discovered there is a purpose to our lives, and we all have unique gifts to share.

My life in the early sixties was what you would likely imagine for those coming into their femininity and womanhood during the decade of "pleasing others." After college, we were to marry. We weren't exactly "Stepford Wives," but we were essentially all the same underneath—women from traditional homes and upbringing with the subliminal narrative and expectation regarding our education, profession, and of course, marriage. The husband was the "good provider," and the wife took care of the children and the house.

I followed my script without question, becoming a teacher and marrying Michael at age twenty-one. I refer to this time as my 'robotic days,' and soon produced two remarkable children, a girl and a boy, fulfilling my destiny. We moved into a house, got the dog too, but when it came to driving a station wagon, I put my foot down.

The late sixties and the seventies were an interesting time, or so I heard. But, unfortunately, my husband and I entirely missed the whole sexual revolution and free-love mindset. Somehow, we weren't invited to the party. I recognize now how much I missed as an impressionable young woman, wife, mother, and professional during the glory days of feminism. I simply never got the memo.

But in the eighties, when my children were older, I went back to get my master's degree in social work. I had always wanted to be a social worker. The eighties proved to be a pivotal period in my life; it became impossible for me to go back to what I thought I knew.

I received an invitation that would change my life entirely. A girlfriend invited me to meet a doctor who was reputed to be able to send healing energy from his chakras to our chakras. I never heard the word "chakra" before, but I was intrigued and wanted to learn more and experience something different.

Now, I can look back at all the life lessons and set intentions that culminated into the most extraordinary transformation of my life. I can see clearly something was calling me to explore the unknown. I was led to pursue this mystery. I didn't understand it at the time, but we live in a world where all things are possible, and there is an organized intelligence supporting all things. My path forward was always right there in front of me, but I was too blind to see my calling—my life purpose.

My life purpose was and is to heal first, from the inside out. Only then could I assist others in finding their unique life purpose—because we all have one.

Thirty-six years ago, I had absolutely no idea what I was in for. But I trusted my calling, my voice, and my guides above, and I listened with patience. I learned to follow my path, my life lesson, my destiny.

> ***"The greatest privilege of a human life is to become a midwife to the awakening of the Soul in another person."***
>
> **~ Plato**

MY STORY

In 1994, I worked with abusive families as a social worker for Family & Children Services. At the time, I did not have a clue about souls, angels, auras, or guides. I was merely following my inner program when I was introduced to healing energy. This was really out of my programmed self. However, it was this first experience that piqued my curiosity and began a journey which is still in process.

Around this time, I was teaching a class called "The Artist's Way" based on the book by Julia Cameron. Though I was learning all about manifesting and angels, I knew nothing about the soul. When I finally started learning about my soul, I realized I had a contribution to make in this world, but I didn't have a clue as to how to go about it.

One morning, as I was writing my morning pages, an exercise from Cameron's book, something incredible happened. For the first time in my life, I experienced what is called automatic writing. This was surprising to me as I heard the words in my mind.

I was startled, yet I had an inner knowledge these words were especially important. But why and how, I did not know. As time went on, I began to trust what I was hearing. I was told to heal myself first and then assist others in their healing process.

At that point, my journey took a significant change of direction. I found that by allowing this inner intelligence to lead, it would provide me with wisdom and unconditional love.

Often, we may experience or encounter extraordinary events, but then self-doubt shows up, and we stop listening to our inner guidance, and fear of the unknown creeps in. This guide is for everyone who has ever wondered why they were born and who they are. I share my transformation in stepping out of my programmed reality and how I tripped, fell flat on my face, picked myself up, and continued on an adventure of a lifetime. This extraordinary journey of healing altered my ordinary life. I went from playing Donna Reed, a mom on an early 1950s television show, to a Transformational Life Coach.

I am honored to share my experiences and lessons learned over the past twenty-seven years. Within this infinite universe, we are always at the right place and the right time in our personal evolution. So, as you begin your journey, know it is through healing yourself that you work toward healing the planet.

I have discovered unseen guides who talk to me all the time; and sure, sometimes they get on my nerves. They have been yelling at me for years to write down my stories, and I have resisted. During the pandemic, with plenty of free time on my hands, I had no more excuses. When going to Traders Joe's is the highlight of my day, I have finally found the time to write my stories.

As I look back on my journey, it's apparent every step I took, every person I met, every lesson I had to learn, and every course I took, all guided me to where I am today. What is also very clear is the universe gives us only what we are ready to learn.

Each of us contains a soul or spirit manifesting unique patterns, lessons, and gifts we bring with us when we are born. But we forget who we are and need to relearn we are here for a purpose. At birth, we are downloaded like a computer program or an app with our parents' beliefs and values. Then, overloading that program or app are our societal and religious beliefs. Now is the time for us to begin to heal and step into a new paradigm—one based on love, not fear. We are here to make history, but we need to heal ourselves first. In every soul's life, a time comes when there is a tap on the shoulder and a call to awaken and fulfill a 'contract.' This is a personal calling.

###

My purpose is to help you see who you are and why you were born, and to ignite the spark of magnificence which lies within your soul.

When you commit yourself to this journey, the gifts you receive are many. Your opportunities and possibilities are limitless. Your journey of self-discovery begins with just one move. It takes the willingness to step out of your preconceived box to experience a new world of unexpected delights. Just yell out, "You-hoo! Is anybody there?" I guarantee your guides and angels will hop off their sofas, throw down their bonbons, and open bottles of champagne. They will be yelling, "Yippee! Let's get started!" The journey is exhilarating!

WHAT IS TRANSFORMATION?

According to Webster's dictionary, ***transformation*** *is an act, process, or instance of transforming or being transformed.* My definition of transformation is first seeking to understand the nature of your life and then allowing the shift in your understanding to affect how you approach your life, how you see others, how you interpret challenges, and what new questions you ask.

By sharing my transformational stories as seeds for you to grow in your own life, I hope to enable you to take steps onto your path of awakening and healing.

I have met many interesting people and have experienced extraordinary life-changing events. I learned my deceased family members, though they passed away a long time ago, were often present in my life when I needed to call on them. I learned I could talk to a six-month-old baby who told me why she had been born, and, on another occasion, I met a little girl who told me her grandfather was her guardian angel. I had many lessons on how to open my heart so love could flow through. I learned how to endure some very scary crises and then watch as the miracles came flooding in. I am now aware life is for you, not against you, and as you heal, you step into an abundance of love and discover why you are here at this particular time.

HOW A PAIR OF FIERCE GERMAN SHEPHERDS AND A MYSTERIOUS FOREIGN DOCTOR CHANGED MY LIFE

When asked what prompted me to step into what many call 'the mysteries,' I always start with the story of the Russian doctor whose name I don't remember. Before I encountered this healer's energy, I was skeptical, judgmental, and self-righteous. I was the stereotypical 1950s and 60s housewife, dressing up to make breakfast, taking my kids to school, doing the laundry, doing the ironing, and serving my husband a good dinner the moment he walked through the door. My pearls were in place, lipstick applied, and I had a smile on my face. This was not always an easy role to play.

There are times in most people's lives when they have an opportunity to step out of what they know to be true into a new and unknown adventure. However, we are often stopped by fear. We stay in stifling careers and relationships.

We say, "No, thank you" to climbing mountains, zip-lining or para-sailing, and exploring the universe. In my case, the object of my fear was neither heights, change, or even the unknown. My fear was much simpler, more concrete, and consisted of two very large, snarling German shepherds.

The story began more than a decade ago. It was a bad time for me, dark and painful. As a social worker for Child Protective Services, I spent my days working with children who had been neglected, abused, or both. I had a huge caseload filled with complex family situations, many of them involving angry and estranged parents, and I found little respite at home. My mother was in the final stage of her life and had moved in with my family, where she needed a great deal of attention. In addition, I was plagued by neck and shoulder aches, probably caused by the stress, although I would not have made this connection at the time.

One day, I received an invitation from a friend, a psychiatric nurse. She and some of her colleagues were attending a healing group with a doctor who was visiting the area. My friend described this doctor as an energy healer who would send healing energy from his aura to those of us in the group. I didn't know what auras were, so I did some research and found out they are emotional, mental, and spiritual levels that form an energy field around the body known as the aura. It was still difficult to conceptualize, and being a big fan of the scientific method, I was skeptical from the outset. After all, I believed if you couldn't prove it, it did not exist.

Even though I had lived in Northern California for years, where these topics were popular in this region, I had little patience with the paranormal or spiritual. Western traditions served me well enough. Yet, at the same time, I was curious. For one thing, attending the healing group would be better than sitting at home and watching television. At worst, I would get a good story out of it. In the remote chance it worked, I had to admit, I could certainly use some healing. So, I said yes.

On the night of the presentation, just finding the house was a nightmare. The neighborhood was extremely wooded and badly lit. Only a sliver of the moon was out that night, and it was too dark to see the house addresses. We arrived late after driving up a lot of wrong driveways. Through the trees, we saw a porch light and began walking up a path of well-worn stones. The air was filled with the fragrance of evergreens.

We were met by two large dogs that did not appear happy to see us. They began barking, then growling and baring their teeth. We walked slowly and with great trepidation, but they were in front of the porch, blocking the entrance. I told my friend we should turn around and leave before we were eaten. My friend looked at me and laughed as she grabbed my arm and pulled me past the dogs and into the house. To this day, I would swear that one dog was ready to take a bite out of me.

Once inside, the house was dark. Flickering candles lit the musty room, and heavy drapes covered the windows. The walls were decorated with religious icons I did not recognize, and a foreign aroma I later learned was incense lingered in the space. The entire setting felt like something from a Grimm's fairy tale. It was creepy, but I was curious, and since the alternative was to head back outside with the dogs, I opted for the living room. There were people in various forms of repose. Some were on the sofa, others on chairs and the floor. We found seats upfront, and the doctor soon entered.

A rather thin man with a full beard, the doctor wore a dark-blue suit and a poorly ironed white shirt. He had very bright eyes and looked kind. Our hostess introduced him. While he sat in front of us, the hostess explained his ability to send healing energy from his aura to other people's auras and that the energy would know where our bodies would need the healing. After her introduction, the room got very quiet, and he began sweeping his hands up and down in patterns as if directing an orchestra. With one eye closed and the other slightly open, I watched as I tried to make sense of what was going on. All of a sudden, I heard a loud voice in my head say, "Lynn, shut your eyes and be quiet." Startled, I thought, "Oh my god, what was that?" I looked around, and it didn't seem to be one of the nurses. So, I surprised myself by doing what I was told to do, shutting both of my eyes and remaining quiet.

Suddenly, a blast of tingling, vibrating energy started running through the core of my body. It first came into the base of my spine, what I now know as my root chakra, and then flowed upward through my entire body. It felt like joyful waves of bubbles as it rose to my head in an explosion of fireworks. There were bright, colorful lights shooting upward in spectacular patterns, followed by feelings of euphoria and a spaciness that bordered on drunkenness. It was nothing like what I expected. I knew deep down within me it was something very profound, even though I couldn't explain it.

After it was over, I sat with my eyes closed as long as I could, trying to savor the experience. Finally, my friend nudged me and told me it was time to go. Everyone else had left, and the doctor had gone to his room. When I stood up, I noticed my sinuses were clear. That in itself was a miracle as I always had allergies, and now, I could breathe. Back in the car, I could not stop talking about what I experienced. Finally, I stopped babbling long enough to ask my friend what she had experienced. "Nothing," she replied. "Oh," was all I could say.

That night marked an inflection point for me. I acquired a sense of peacefulness and inner joy I had never experienced before, but it also left me wanting to learn more and to make sense of what had happened. Something deep inside me had awakened. I was ready for whatever life wanted to bring to me next. I was willing to go beyond my borders of beliefs and fears. This was the beginning of my life-changing adventure. I didn't realize it at the time, but this beginning experience opened my mind.

I was intrigued, and needed to explore and learn more about healing energy. So, what did I do? I took off the pearls and apron and stepped into a new adventure. Goodbye traditional housewife, here comes a new adventure!

###

Today, I work as a transformational life coach. My mother has long since passed away, and my house is again a place of refuge. I still work with abused children on occasion, but I also work with adults in need of healing by helping them find peace emotionally as well as spiritually. I believe we all have free will to choose the course of our lives, yet I know often unrelated events and experiences line up in meaningful ways to take us on a new journey. There are many teachers, doctors, friends, and healers I want to thank for guiding me on this path, as well as a pair of fierce, snarling German shepherds who propelled me through the door.

THE NEXT BABY STEP: LEARNING ABOUT ENERGY

The energy I experienced that evening was so powerful I was eager to learn more. The universe always listens, and an opportunity presented itself. Michael, my husband, was invited to Chile to study with a renowned Chilean physical therapist, so I tagged along.

One day at this seminar, I talked about my experience with energy with one of the physical therapists. He told me he also used energy healing in his physical therapy practice. He said he was able to send healing energy to patients even if they were in a different room. His patients reported feeling vibrations in the parts of their bodies that needed healing. He believes energy is a great healing tool and added how energy vibrations have been measured by instruments at the hospital where he works.

When he asked if I would like to receive energy, of course, I said, "Yes." He became quiet and raised his hand above my head. I felt warm and loving energy vibrations wash all over my body. I loved the feeling then and still do; it will always be magical. It feels like bubbles bursting with joy. Once again, I was intrigued by this invisible vibration, and I was hooked. There was something out there. I wanted to know more.

HERE IS WHERE THE CHAMPAGNE BOTTLE OPENED

After returning home from Chile, I decided I was going to learn as much as I could about this healing energy. So, I made a grand announcement at work; I declared and set my intention I would become spiritual in two years. Although laughter and snarky remarks followed when I made that declaration, my spirituality greatly awakened in those two years. And thankfully, this was just the tip of the iceberg. There was so much more I needed and wanted to learn and, I am still in the process of learning. At this time in my life, I had absolutely no clue a team of guides was listening to me. Once I declared my intention, my guides hopped off the couch and got busy.

Why is setting your intentions so very powerful? Read on.

THE LESSON OF SETTING INTENTIONS

When you launch an objective such as, "I want to be spiritual in two years," you don't have to know anything or do anything for it to happen. You only need to be fully present. By setting your intentions, you are sending a clear message to the universe. I didn't have a clue I was being listened to, but I set the intention, and the roller coaster started.

SETTING ANOTHER INTENTION...

Writing this book of teaching memories has been another adventure as well as an intention. I am a storyteller. I love telling stories; it's the writing of the story that is difficult for me. But I set my intention. I tell stories to plant seeds of awakening, and then I step aside. In the end, it is always up to the listeners and readers to open up and to ask themselves what their journey is revealing. One thing I am certain of: we are always heard, and we are answered by angels, guides, or something else. I know with certainty—we are always answered. Sometimes, we don't get the answer we want, but a lesson is always involved. Sometimes, we are just too unconscious to hear or see the answers.

Write down your intentions. What do you want for your life?

OUR LIFE STORIES ARE OUR TEACHERS

We all have stories from our early years that play a prominent part in developing our thoughts, beliefs, and feelings. In addition, there are many stories we carry deep within our hearts. In the painful stories, we try to protect ourselves from further injury. We place a veil over our hearts. However, it is only when we unveil our hearts and come to the realization that love is more powerful than fear that we can truly love one another and ourselves.

Life is filled with many lessons, and healing requires you, finding the pony in the pile of manure. A long time ago, there was a father and two sons. One of the sons was a pessimist, and the other was an optimist, and the father decided to test his children. So, one day, he put one son in a room filled with manure and his other son in a different room filled with manure. An hour later, he went to see how the boys were doing; his son, the pessimist, was miserable about only being given manure and expressed his distaste to his father; the son who was the optimist cheerfully told his father with so much manure in the room, there had to be a pony someplace. This is a valuable lesson. When life hands you manure, always look for the pony.

Lessons are always opportunities to grow. The lessons you don't like always teach you the most about yourself. If you don't get the lesson the first time, I guarantee it will come back around until you "get it."

One of my biggest lessons was accepting that I do not have control over what happens in my life. I had a difficult time with this lesson, and it gets repeated often as I still need to work on it even now. The only control I have is my attitude. Sometimes, I still forget that.

"Live life as if everything is rigged in your favor."

~ Rumi

MY AWAKENING PROCESS CONTINUES

Returning to California from Chile, I knew I had a mission—to find out more about this healing work. A friend told me about a channeler coming to the Bay Area the following week. What is a channeler? According to Merriam-Webster, the definition of channeler is: a person who conveys thoughts or energy from a source believed to be outside the person's body or conscious mind specifically: one who speaks for nonphysical beings or spirits.

My friend had observed this person before and said her vibrations were loving and powerful. It sounded intriguing. I remembered hearing about channeling in the 80s when I started reading the Seth Material.

The Seth Material is a collection of writing dictated by Jane Roberts to her husband from late 1963 until her death in 1984. Roberts claimed the words were spoken by a discarnate entity named Seth. These books were instrumental in bringing the idea of channeling to a broad public audience.

I was fascinated by Seth's beliefs, but I stopped reading when he presented the concept of "no time," in which he explained our whole lives are occurring at once. At this point, I could not understand what he was talking about, and I couldn't go any further.

The night of the channeling, I went to the address I had. However, it was an apartment building, and I didn't know the apartment number or the name of the person hosting the event. I checked my paper with the address and looked around the street to see if anyone else might be going to see a channeler. But no one was on the street. Finally, out of desperation and about to go home, I said out loud, "If I am supposed to attend this channeling session, please give me a sign." No sooner had I uttered those words than a woman with a yoga pillow came walking down the street. I knew she was going to hear the channeler. There was my sign, so I followed her.

There were about ten people in the living room when Teresa, the channeler, emerged from the back bedroom and introduced herself. She told the group she is referred to as an out-of-body channeler. She explained how she goes into a trance and communicates through an entity called Sarasvati. She returned to the bedroom and when she came out again, she was now Sarasvati, the Hindu goddess of learning, wisdom, music, and aesthetics. When Teresa came back out of the bedroom, something was different about her. Her presence felt much larger and more loving. My body started to vibrate in her presence; I felt as if tiny champagne bubbles were bursting open. It was remarkable. There was the same energy again. I had such a great time that evening I immediately signed up for the class she was giving the next day. I was both intrigued and scared.

In the second class, I felt a huge pop that vibrated throughout my body. It was loud, and everyone heard it. I wasn't scared but super curious. Later, I learned what popped was my root chakra, and I was told that it had opened. I didn't have a clue what was happening, but it was forceful. Teresa channeling Sarasvati was powerful, and I decided the next time she came to the Bay Area, I would see her again. I wanted her to give God a message from me.

COMPLAINING TO GOD

At this time, I felt Sarasvati was as close as I could get to God. I didn't feel as if I had any power, and I wanted to complain about how the children on Earth were being treated.

I decided I was going to have a one-on-one session to complain to God. In my mind, I wanted Sarasvati to report to God; I never realized for a moment I also had a connection.

I was in a quandary on the day of the session. What do you wear when you complain to God? I must have gone through half of my closet before I finally decided on an outfit. What should I say? How would my complaints be received? I could not stop the thousands of butterflies in my stomach. I was angry, and I wanted God to hear me. I sat in the room, waiting patiently for Teresa to arrive. When she came in and asked me why I was there, I blurted out the reason I had come to see her. Sarasvati listened carefully to me and acknowledged what I was saying. She began to tell me everyone is born for a reason and it is not my job to judge another's journey. You must come from a place within your heart that is filled with love and compassion, not from judgment.

Judgment is not our job. We do not walk in the footsteps of others, she said, and we do not know the lessons they are to receive. After paying $125.00 to complain to God, she told me I had a direct connection and didn't need anyone else. I left feeling I was heard, and I felt better and less angry. (As a family and child social worker, I had the experience of being a witness to some extremely disturbing cases, and I have to say it took longer to leave anger and judgment behind, but I eventually did.)

MY FIRST SPIRITUAL WOMEN'S GROUP

I loved teaching and sharing what I was learning. I started a women's group, primarily coworkers and friends who were interested in spirituality. We met once a month with different speakers, activities, lunch, and socialization included. In retrospect, I think most of the women came for the lunch and socialization part.

One Saturday, a member of the group brought a guest speaker who was a Reiki master. In her presentation, she told us that Reiki means, 'spiritually guided life force energy.' 'Rei' means God's wisdom or the higher power and 'ki' is 'life force energy.' It is a method of healing thousands of years old which originated in Japan. So, of course, I was interested in anything that used energy, which got my undivided attention.

The Reiki master told us the healing modality had previously only been taught in Japan and was recently introduced in the United States by her teacher, Mrs. Takata. After the introduction to Reiki, she then demonstrated the technique. Once again, I experienced a surge of warm energy from her hands. No sooner had I experienced this than I knew I wanted to learn how to work with this kind of energy. I signed up on the spot to take the first-degree training.

FIRST-DEGREE REIKI TRAINING

There were six women in my training class which taught us the basics of energy healing for oneself and how to use Reiki on others. After a brief lecture, the teacher showed us the Reiki symbols used in the practice. Next, we all formed a circle and shut our eyes as the teacher proceeded to walk around each chair, giving what I later learned were Reiki attunements to each student. The purpose of the attunements is to open the students' ability to channel Reiki energy.

WAS I ANOINTED BY JESUS?

As I was receiving the attunement, I felt an energy pulse like a stream of warm liquid flowing on my head. I also felt Jesus's presence in the room. I knew he was there, and I knew he had poured something warm and loving on the top of my head. There I was, a Jewish girl feeling Jesus pour something on my head! OMG. This took my breath away. How could this be? But I knew it was true deep inside.

We shared our experiences of what we felt. I told the group I felt the presence of Jesus and he had poured something on my head. The teacher said she also felt his presence and he was anointing us. I didn't know what anointing was all about. But I have to say, his presence felt so comforting. I wondered how my family would take the news.

We then practiced using our new-found skills on one another. The heat pouring from my hands was so strong I thought something was wrong. The energy was intense. The person I worked on had shoulder pain and after about ten minutes, the pain was gone. I went home with a new story and a new healing tool for assisting my beloved dog. As Reiki initiates in training, we learned the words and symbols first. More importantly, I learned to set my intention to connect with God's source energy, letting its flow move through me. If this worked on people, why wouldn't it work on my fifteen-year-old dog's bladder cancer? I loved this dog so much I would try to give her the energy I was learning to provide. Every night I blasted her with the healing energy, and she lived for two more years. I was beyond thrilled.

Since then, I have realized energy is a magical life force, and its job is to heal us. It is the language the body speaks. There is a movie, a documentary that shows so clearly how our thoughts, feelings, and beliefs about ourselves can alter our bodies.

"WHAT THE BLEEP DO WE KNOW?"

In 2004, a wonderful inspirational documentary, What The Bleep Do WE Know? was released starring Marlee Matlin as a divorced photographer whose experiences are incredible when life begins to unravel around her, revealing the cellular, molecular, and quantum worlds that lie beneath everything.

I remember two very powerful messages I learned from this documentary. The first one was Dr. Emoto's research. He took water samples from extremely polluted rivers and then froze the samples. They were so ugly and malformed when viewed under the microscope. Then he took these samples and asked monks to pray over them. One monk would pray with love, another in gratitude, another with compassion and so forth. When the water samples were placed under the microscope again, the ugly crystals from the polluted water turned into magnificent new crystal patterns that looked like snowflakes. They were all different from each other, but all were brilliant in design and color. This experiment showed how thoughts, words, and prayers all affected the water crystals. It illustrates how one's thoughts can affect the molecules in one's body, and we are composed of seventy percent water.

In the film's last scenes, Marlee Matlin is upset and sitting in a bathtub writing all over her body, "I hate you; I hate you; I hate you." Then something clicks and she remembers the research done by Dr. Emoto. She then quickly changes and writes on her body, "I love you; I love you; I love you." How many of us during our lives have said these words to our bodies? Usually, we say other things and often wonder why men don't have fat thighs.

Another remarkable part of this movie was how it portrayed addiction. It was probably the best work I've ever seen on really getting what addiction looks like in a body. This film is so powerful I recommend it to all of you. I also recommend Dr. Emoto's book, The Hidden Messages in Water.

BELIEFS

> ***"The world as we have created it is a process of our thinking. It cannot be changed without changing our thinking."***
>
> **~ Albert Einstein**

Everything starts with what we believe it to be. Our thoughts create our reality. One of my greatest discoveries was that I was the co-creator of my life. Who knew! My thoughts were creating my experiences! If I kept choosing the martyr role or the victim role, I would call in these experiences that reinforced my unconscious thoughts. Not a good idea, especially the painful, broken-hearted experiences.

You get what you believe to be true, even if you don't know a belief system is running you. Not accepting or understanding I had chosen to experience certain events—despite how my choices made me feel badly about myself—had kept me in a vicious cycle. I am thankful I finally "got it" and I don't have to play that game anymore.

One of the simplest and greatest spiritual principles I learned was from a Course in Miracles. The Course in Miracles says whenever we suffer, experience loss or fear, or are dissatisfied with the outcome of a given event, it is because the outcome was what we thought we deserved. All of this is at an unconscious level of what we believe to be true about ourselves. Therefore, it is only when we become conscious of what we are thinking and projecting that we can then change.

I have met many individuals who get stuck in their life stories. They keep repeating these stories until they get it. In most of the relationships of people I've worked with, they call in another person after they left the first one thinking this person will be phenomenal, and all they get is the same person they just left, only with different shoes.

Until you start the journey of healing yourself and your belief systems, you will not attract anybody at a higher vibration than you are. When you start working on your wounds looking back as an adult and realizing these wounds—issues that come up from your childhood—should not be running your life anymore, you become more enlightened and can change the trajectory. With this new alignment, you will grow and attract the people you want to have in your life. But until then, you keep getting the same person repeatedly wearing different shoes.

Get a notepad and sit quietly.

Observe and write down any reoccurring patterns that show up in your life.

For example, my unconscious belief that I was not enough kept calling in the same situations where I felt I wasn't enough.

Now would be a good time to write down your beliefs. Answer some of these questions. See if you can find your core beliefs and don't judge them. Just look at them. They have so much information for you, and they're basically all unconscious.

The belief that life can be good and loving gets us

moving in the right direction. As we see we are having an impact on our reality, our belief expands to trusting and developing faith in ourselves.

As this new Belief grows, we Trust more, and what a real eye-opener that leads to developing more Faith in ourselves.

Believe. Trust. Faith.

The first step is awareness.

THE POWER OF EARLY WOUNDS

What are the hidden messages we tell ourselves and where do they come from?

In my healing, I had to deal with self-esteem continuously through the process.

I had to look at my superficial and deep wounds and how I saw myself. The deeper you dig, the more you find.

I now know negative as well as positive thoughts impact not only our bodies but our minds. They are electromagnetic. I always say to others, "Your thoughts create your experiences. They are energy." But I never realized the thoughts acquired in childhood could have such a powerful effect on what we are trying to manifest.

If I have a negative thought sitting in my unconscious mind it directly impacts the experiences I encounter. I discovered our bodies are always listening to our thoughts. So, we get what we think about ourselves, even if what we get are subconscious thoughts.

MY STORY

I wanted to lead a workshop. I studied for many years, and I was a big sponge absorbing all of the fascinating healing information. After some time, I was ready to start working with small groups. I enjoyed working with others, and I was good at it, and I was funny. I was ready to tackle a bigger project. Or so I thought. I prepared the entire workshop and believed it was as good as it could be. It had my teachings, meditations, stories, and even an art project. Finally, I was ready to launch. I sent out flyers, emails, asked my friends for support, and publicized the workshop in the local newspaper. Then it happened.

Two people showed up for the workshop. I was devastated. That's when my ugliest thought came up from deep in the unconscious mind. The thought was: "I'm not good enough, I'm never going to succeed. There are so many others brighter and better than I am." I can see now what happened, but then I just thought I was not good enough. With my negative thinking, I shot down my dreams. This was a huge lesson and provided another great healing opportunity for growth.

MY DEEP WOUNDS ARE BORN

Here are how some of my childhood deep wounds were born. What I know for sure is we all come from the scar clan. Some of us have our scars outside, and most of us have our scars inside. Although most of our beliefs about ourselves start when we are small children, I knew I wasn't enough even at three years old. How does this happen? Read on.

THE SCAR CLAN

It is important to remember babies are totally reliant on caregivers for everything. They are helpless and cannot survive on their own. Studies show babies will die when they're not held and comforted. It's not just about food and diaper changes. What matters most is love. Values and beliefs are passed down from generation to generation. The cycle of sexual abuse, alcohol, and physical abuse are all passed down. We look at the world as a friendly place or a world that is scary, depending on how we have been raised and the experiences we had as children. These experiences usually happen at an unconscious level and keep repeatedly repeating until they are seen and understood. You can only change your story and create a brand-new movie when you can see what is happening and why it is that way.

There are many lessons on how early-life experiences can be so powerful that we keep on recreating the same situations in our lives. As in my case, I was not enough and something was wrong with me. We have the beliefs, religious values, and attitudes of our parents and society imprinted on us without our awareness. How you were disciplined as a child is often how you will discipline your own children. How your parents were in their relationship is your teacher. What I know for sure is we all come from the 'scars' clan. Some wear their scars on the outside, and some wear their scars on the inside. In working with adults, I always start by listening to their beliefs and their attitudes about the world. You simply have to listen closely to a person to hear what he or she believes is true and how that individual has created a life based on these beliefs.

There was a radio program in the 90s on NPR called "Paul Harvey and the News." I always liked to listen as he would share a story and then break for a commercial. Then, when he returned, he would say, "Now, here is the rest of the story." So, when I listen closely to a person's beliefs, I will then say, "Now here is the rest of your story."

Some of the wounds we carry with us from childhood include:

I am not enough.

I'm invisible.

I am alone.

I am not lovable.

I don't matter.

These beliefs show up in our lives, usually at an unconscious level. As a result, they keep us playing small. However, they are not true beliefs, and after you see what they really are, you can develop new skills and be the producer, the director, and the star of a new movie.

MY BIG WOUND

I was born on a sunny, spring day in Chicago, Illinois. If I must say so myself, I was an adorable little girl with curly, blond hair and hazel eyes. I weighed 7 pounds 4 ounces and was 19 inches long. I realize now that was the thinnest I was ever going to be. My birth announcement compared me to a car with rear and front bumpers, taillights, and a loud horn. I am glad my father liked cars.

At the time of my birth, my mother was thirty-seven years old, and my father was fifty-three. I was the second child born three years after my mother had given birth to a baby boy who had strangled on the umbilical cord. This had to be devastating to my parents, who waited three years before they decided to have another baby.

I found out we are all born with a blueprint, and in a seminar led by Deepak Chopra, I found out I was born as a protector.

In my early spiritual days, I was in a seminar led by Deepak Chopra with about 500 people. He had just taken us into a deep meditation. In this meditation, I saw myself floating in my mother's womb. In the womb, I could see light, veins, and murky water. I had a burning need to let my mother know I would be all right and not to worry. I felt a keen sense of awareness of my physical surroundings and the fear in my mother's body. As hard as I tried to comfort her worries, I couldn't. This was an incredibly powerful meditation for me. So, it is interesting when reflecting back on my life, I was always the protector in my family, and I even went on to become a family and child social worker who worked with abused children. I am a Mama Bear!

The rest of the story is my parents lived in an apartment building, and I was the only child in the building. I was adored. I can remember clearly playing with my parent's friends, who I called aunt and uncle. Aunt Peggy lived next door, and I would go to her apartment, where she had a little chair and table set up just for me. I didn't know it at the time, but she was a kept woman. Being able to wear her furry and feathery bedjackets and her fluffy slippers was grand!

I would dress up in her silk bed jackets and slippers, and we would play. My mother used to tell the story of how I rebelled at age two-and-a-half. She said I was at Aunt Peggy's apartment, and as it was time for dinner, she came over to get me. I refused to go and said I wanted to stay. I was a very stubborn two-year-old exerting my power. She then threatened if I didn't go home, she would take my clothes off as that was how I came to her. The threat did not motivate me. I liked Aunt Peggy's clothes more.

Then she threatened to take all of my toys and throw them in the incinerator. I went home for dinner, and the power struggle was over. I lost. From birth until age three, I played with loving adults, and they catered to my every whim. I was the hit of the building. Then it was time for nursery school. I remember being so excited as I waited for the bus to take me to school—my first time playing with other children.

WHAT HAPPENED NEXT WAS A DEEP WOUND THAT LASTED A LONG TIME

Looking back on my early life stories, I can see how specific patterns were created, which continued into my adult life. When injured, our hearts can shut down. It is only by reflecting upon the stories in our past that we can see the patterns that keep coming up again and again, with absolutely no true awareness of where they originated. The 'not feeling good enough' and 'not feeling smart enough' starts in our early childhood. Even heartbreak begins there. Since our thoughts create our reality, it is no wonder we keep reliving similar experiences and recreating the same pain that has been deeply buried and yet arises once again from the wells of our subconscious. It is only when we can truly see it, and acknowledge its presence, that we can choose whether or not to let the pain control us. With these wounds of our childhood, it is amazing how we still can consciously evolve, healing and growing into healthy and happy adults. I read ninety percent of our thoughts are unconscious and ten percent are conscious. We all need to pay attention to our thoughts. After all, who is driving the car? "I'm not enough" is the message that was born.

Getting off the yellow bus and stepping into the new school was a life-changing experience for my three-year-old self. I could barely contain my excitement. As I opened the door, I saw life-sized wooden blocks, bikes, wagons, toys, easels for painting, and then the very best thing—a life-sized dollhouse. The dollhouse was equipped with a stove, refrigerator, sink, doll bunk beds, dolls, doll clothing, dishes, and a small table and four chairs. It was everything I loved at age three—playing house.

Until I started telling the other children playing in the dollhouse what to do. I was used to being a boss, but obviously, that did not serve me in this situation. The other children would not play with me, and I didn't have any tools to cope with this situation, as I had never played with other children before.

My first friend in nursery school was Miss Jane, one of the teachers. As a three-year-old child, you cannot conceptualize the reasons as to why a situation may happen. I just thought something was wrong with me. I carried this thought for a long time in relationships with others. This wound was powerful and buried deep within the unconscious mind, yet operating all the time. So, I tried to be different and looked at others to see how they were. Sometimes, it worked; other times, it did not.

NEXT WOUND, DUMPED AT CAMP

While at a workshop with Hank Wesselman, Ph.D., I received the gift of becoming aware of my guide's presence as a witness to the pain I felt in the experience of my first love ditching me. I was twelve years old when I had the good fortune of going to a boy-and-girl sleep-away camp in Wisconsin. I didn't know anyone else going and was brave all the way up until my mom and dad brought me to the train station.

At that moment, I realized I was leaving my family. Panic set in, and I started to cry. Finally, the camp director saw what was happening and whisked me away, put me on the train, and off I went on an unknown adventure.

I was introduced to the other girls who were in my cabin, and life felt good again. Camp was wonderful. Every Saturday night, there was a dance with the girls staying on one side of the room and the boys on the other. There, I stood with my cabin mates when a cute boy asked me to dance, and then another one asked. I was overjoyed. I must admit I was boy crazy. At the first dance, one boy, Mike, asked me to dance over and over again. I immediately fell for him. I was twelve, and he was older, maybe thirteen. After the last dance, Mike asked if he could walk me back to the halfway road, the road separating the boy's and girl's camp. I was thrilled and, of course, agreed. I felt butterflies throughout my body, up and down. Being walked back to my cabin by a boy was the most excitement I had ever felt. Oh, my goodness! And then he kissed me. I could hardly breathe. It was my very first kiss, and I liked it. We kissed again. Bliss! I wrote my mom to let her know a boy had kissed me, and I asked her to send me my first bra.

I looked forward to Saturday night dances as I knew Mike would dance only with me, walk me back to the halfway road, and kiss me. Then to my dismay—what I term "the event"—happened. Several Saturday nights later, my cabin mates and I went to the dance, but Mike did not ask me to dance that night. He didn't walk me back to the halfway road, and there was no more kissing. I was devastated. What had I done? I was at a loss. I danced with other boys, but I walked back to my cabin alone, crying the entire way.

Though I had no idea what depression looked like at the time, I was depressed. I couldn't eat or sleep. I cried all the time. Though one of my cabin counselors did listen to my woes, it didn't help me feel any better. My heart hurt, and I was in pain. Ditched at twelve. Looking back, I can smile, but at the time, I was devastated.

At the end of the camp season, there was a cotillion, and everyone dressed up for the last dance. Out of the blue, Mike asked me to go with him to the dance. I immediately said yes, thinking everything was back to normal. For that evening, it was perfect. We danced, and he walked me back to the halfway point, and he kissed me. He also said he would save a seat on the train for me, but he didn't. Heartbreak again, and I didn't even get a chance to say goodbye.

I relived this twelve-year-old camp romance trauma/drama during a workshop with Hank Wesselman, Ph.D. He led the group into a deep meditation, where this entire experience replayed in my head. I found myself back at camp as a twelve-year-old. The tears were streaming down my face as I remember how I felt. What had I done wrong? Obviously, this unconscious experience needed to be healed. Then I noticed my guide, Aaron, standing next to me. He had witnessed my pain and depression. I can't explain how healing it is to know someone else witnessed my pain, even if it is an unseen guide. It was comforting, and I remember asking in the meditation, "Aaron, you were there, too?" And the answer was, "Yes." It was then I felt a cloak of relief wash over me. That was the gift.

Though I don't know where Mike is today, I'm grateful for all my experiences, especially the gift of becoming more aware of the loving presence of my guide being there with me. But if I saw Mike today, the twelve-year-old girl in me would want to kick him in the shin.

MORE WOUNDS

I was twelve-and-a-half years old when my father passed away suddenly on December 4, 1956. My brother and I were not taught how to mourn. I am sure we both cried, but I do not remember doing so. I think I was just stunned and didn't realize what a loss this would be. Everyone appeared to act as they normally would, and we never saw anyone cry. My entire life changed on that devastating day.

In 1971, my friend's husband took a seminar called EST. He would not divulge any information about this seminar. All we knew was it was a two-weekend training (sixty hours) held in a San Francisco hotel, and participants could not get up to go to the bathroom. No matter how my friend and I prodded him, he wouldn't say anything. I hate being left out. So, my friend and I decided to see what this was all about. I vowed to tell everyone interested about my experience. Not knowing what I was getting into but thrilled at the new adventure, off we went.

The seminar leader would conduct something called processes. These processes all started with meditation and relaxation techniques, accompanied by soothing music. As soon as the participants were in a meditative state, the trainer would interject questions. I had never experienced a process before, but it was wonderful.

One of the mornings after the trainer relaxed the 250 people in the audience, he asked, "What would you say to someone living or dead if you had the chance?" Wow! That question hit me like a ton of bricks, and immediately my response was, "Why did you die?" I never really dealt with my father's death. When I heard the trainer ask the question, I had an immediate reaction in my body. My eyes welled with tears, and my nose started to run. I was warm and trying to stuff all my feelings back down where they came from, way deep inside. I was so busy trying to suppress my feelings I didn't hear the next questions asked. But I heard the last one, "What do you give up by not communicating what you want to say to that person living or dead?" Right away, inside my head I heard, "You give up your aliveness." I sat in utter amazement as I did not know how it came to me, but I knew I would have to stand up and share what happened.

The process was over, and the trainer said, "Does anyone wish to share?" I raised my hand. Someone came over with a microphone, and there I stood in front of the crowds of people crying, with my nose running and no Kleenex. I was a mess. The trainer asked me what I wanted to share. I told him about my father's death, and how what had come up for me was the question, "Why did you die?" The trainer then asked, "Lynn, did your father love you?" I said, "He came home for dinner every night and brought us candy."

He repeated the question, "Lynn, did your father love you?" I must have spent five minutes saying, "I don't know." In EST, you either love someone, or you don't; there is no 'I don't know.' Finally, after asking me the question numerous times, he emphatically said in a firm voice, "Lynn, did your father love you?" I responded finally with the word, "Yes."

He then said, "Lynn, do you think your father died on purpose?" And I must admit, as a twelve-year-old, I did. I thought he died on purpose. He died, and we had to move. I went to a new school, and my mother, a stay-at-home mother, now went to work. I shared a bedroom with my mother and watched over my nine-year-old brother, who was a challenge.

He went on to say if there was anything I needed to do, it was to apologize to my father for thinking he died on purpose. I sat down and felt a huge weight being lifted off my shoulders.

I told my husband and friends what transpired and how good I felt. I know there is some bad press about EST, but for me, it was a gift. It introduced me to ideas of personal responsibility, accountably, and the beginning of my transformation.

ANOTHER WOUND THAT HAD A GREAT ENDING

Life changed dramatically after the death of my father. Our family had lived in a three-bedroom, two-bath apartment on the South Side of Chicago. My brother and I each had our own bedrooms. My room was painted pink, and the bedspreads on my twin beds matched. I loved my bedroom and had a lot of friends who lived nearby since I had grown up there from the age of five to twelve. After my dad passed away, my mother went to work full time, taking over his business, a men's wholesale clothing store in the city. As a result, we moved out to the suburbs and into a small duplex apartment with two bedrooms and one bath in which I shared a bedroom with my mother. My mother picked this area as we were given lunch each day at our new school. This was a blessing for my mother as she worked from 9:00 a.m. to 6:00 p.m. every day except Sundays, and on Sundays, she prepared food for us for the entire week. She made the meals, and I warmed them up and made a salad. I remember I always started our dinner off with Ritz crackers and cheese as I thought that was so sophisticated and either chocolate or butterscotch pudding for dessert. I must have made this countless times before my mother asked me if we could have a different dessert.

I started at a different school for eighth grade, and again I felt lost and alone. The cliques had already been formed a long time before I got there. There was a rainbow on the horizon when two new eighth-grade girls moved to the school a month later. I was overjoyed. The three of us became best friends and are still best friends to this day, sixty-three years later. They are my soul sisters, Sandy and Renee. We love and support each other. They were and still are my gifts.

AARON ON MY WOUNDS

Aaron is my spiritual guide and has provided me with many lessons on this journey. I found this message in my 2000 notes:

"What is going on with you? You are being offered a wonderful opportunity to take a good look at yourself. To see what your blocks are and what has run them for the past years. It is all about observing, seeing what's really in your head, and seeing you are not that person, the person you always thought you were. You are beautiful, smart, and kind. You have more to give, and do not let that block continue, or you will cut off the best part of you. Let it go. It is not reality. It is merely a perceived thought process you have used for most of your life. No one is better or worse than another. Everyone has blocks, worries, and fears. It is not wise to stay attached to old wounds. It serves no purpose."

A GIFT FROM MY FATHER TWENTY YEARS LATER

It was exactly twenty years after I had taken the EST training when my father answered me.

At this time, I followed all the suggestions and opportunities to continue exploring my spirituality. I had an opportunity to book an appointment with Hans Christian King, a psychic medium.

As I got off the elevator, Mr. King was standing in the hallway waiting for me with a big smile. He looked as if he were a kind and sweet grandfather. Even before we walked into the room, he said, "There is a father figure standing near you throwing bouquets of flowers all over you saying, 'Tell my daughter I love her. Tell my daughter I love her.'" Mr. King then asked me if my father was living or deceased. I told him my father died when I was twelve years old. Mr. King said my father insisted on saying over and over again, "Tell my daughter I love her."

Twenty years earlier in the EST seminar, I was asked if my father loved me. At the time, I said, "I don't know." Now, here in this moment twenty years later with Hans Christian King, my father was telling me he loved me. It was mind-blowing. I was told many things that afternoon, but what I remember most is that my father came through and said he loved me. That was the gift. I was learning I was being listened to on a higher level and would get answers, though not when I might expect them. This was my first encounter with being answered, and it was sensational.

I left the session feeling higher than a kite with another story to tell. Mr. King also referred me to a friend of his who was a spiritual coach.

Due to my early childhood wounding, I spent the next forty years trying to fit into groups. I was a square peg trying so hard to fit into a round hole. But, of course, I didn't realize I had a deep wound of not being enough operating at an unconscious level in those moments. These unconscious beliefs call to you what you believe to be true about yourself. It's a vicious cycle.

I had to work on healing this wound of not feeling pretty enough, smart enough, or clever enough. I learned we are all unique beings with extraordinary gifts. It is a huge part of awakening to who you really are. For me, it was time to stop the movie. I don't play small anymore, and I am proud to be a square peg.

"You teach best what you most need to learn."

~ Richard Bach, Illusions

WHEN THE TEACHER IS READY; MY FIRST TEACHING GIG

A Rabbi, A Book, Two Jews, and Sixteen Reformed Catholics.

I had a lot more to learn. In one of my classes, a student once asked how I got started with teaching spirituality classes. I laughed as I remembered exactly what the motivating impetus was for my first class. It was a Rabbi, a book, two Jews, and sixteen reformed Catholics that began my spiritual teaching career. There is a saying, "When the student is ready, the teacher appears." It is also true for a teacher. "When a teacher is ready, the students appear." It all started when Rabbi Raskin, my temple rabbi whom I adored, asked me if I would consider teaching a class on spirituality. I shared with him some of the new insights I was learning and experiencing. I had just begun my spiritual quest. What did I know about teaching a class on spirituality? Not much. But I didn't hesitate, not even for a moment. What was I thinking? The reason I uttered the word "yes" was the result of an intention I made to the universe in 1994. I might have forgotten the intention for a moment, but back then, after reading a few books on spirituality and having some out-of-the-box experiences, I took a stand. I declared aloud to everyone who would listen that I wanted to become spiritual in two years. I immediately began this journey, looking through all the spiritual books and notes I had accumulated. Attempting to gather material to put together in a class outline, I became more and more confused. This in turn, led to becoming more certain I knew nothing.

At this point, I began sitting and praying for some guidance. The Rabbi called to see how I was doing with my preparation for the class. I confessed I was drowning in a sea of spiritual confusion. It was then he sent me a life preserver. He said, "Lynn, weren't you the person who recommended I buy the book The Artist's Way by Julia Cameron?" "Yes," I said. "Well," he began, "Then teach from that book." It never crossed my mind, even though I had taken a class based on this book. I was saved.

The proverbial net had appeared. The temple placed notices in the bulletin as well as the local newspapers. The day before the class began, I phoned the temple office to see how many individuals had registered. Out of a congregation of 1,500 people, only two members had signed up for the class. That news would burst anyone's bubble. While wishing more people had signed up, I was still determined to teach this class regardless of how many came. The evening of the first class found me in a state of nervous excitement. I couldn't eat, and my heart was racing. The class was in the library, and the library had just been remodeled and the smell of fresh paint, new carpet, and old books permeated the room. The only sound in the room, aside from my breathing, was the ticking of the wall clock announcing to me the time was getting closer for my class to begin. It felt like thousands of butterflies were doing the tango in my stomach. I must have checked my notes a hundred times as I waited. I looked up, saw a man at the door, and he asked if this is where the spirituality class was meeting. I flew off my chair to welcome him with a silent prayer of thanks. Then another person showed up, and then more began arriving. There was noise and laughter in the library. Eighteen people arrived and were now sitting around the library table. I took a deep breath and realized I was the leader of this class. Now what? It was time to step up to the plate. The class was well underway when the Rabbi poked his head into the room to see how the class was going. He winked at me and gave me one of his warm and generous smiles. I smiled back. No one could have predicted my first spirituality class at the temple would be composed of two Jewish women and sixteen reformed Catholics.

As I drove home, still filled with the excitement of that first class, I noticed there was a full moon. I pulled my car over and howled at the moon. How was I to know this first experience would set off a chain of events whereby I would eventually become a Transformational Life Coach?

LEARNING ABOUT MANIFESTING

Have you ever thought about someone with whom you haven't spoken to in a while, and then the phone rings, and it's that person? You're amazed because it is the exact person you were thinking about. Or, have you ever been looking for a book, and it suddenly falls off the shelf at your feet? Are these coincidences, happy accidents, or just 'wow' experiences? I've come to believe these are examples of a mysterious force called synchronicity—an experience of two or more unrelated events occurring together in a meaningful manner. It is a concept first described by Swiss Psychologist Carl Jung as, "meaningful coincidences that seem to have no causal relationship, except to the person who experiences them." Every culture acknowledges synchronicity but calls it by different names. It has been labeled coincidence, luck, fate, omens, destiny, karma, miracles, chance, intuition, and serendipity. In my experiences, I have found it to be both powerful and joyful. I first experienced 'synchronicity' when I began facilitating my first spiritual group based on Julia Cameron's book, The Artist's Way. We had just finished reading about synchronicity in week one, and the very next week, everyone was so excited to report they started recognizing and experiencing synchronistic events.

One student said, the perfect sofa she wanted had been reduced to a price she could afford. Another was searching for a skirt to go with the top she'd bought a while back and was told there were none. The kindly salesperson offered to go to the stockroom just to check, and lo and behold, the skirt, in the right size, had just been returned. Another student in the group was looking for a new job, went to a dinner party, and was seated next to a very nice person who offered to help her find a job. As for myself, I asked for some inexpensive, pale-yellow towels; they showed up in Costco the next time I went. Wow, I was so excited and overjoyed. I kept telling my daughter, "Do you see those pale-yellow towels? I asked for them!" She thought I had absolutely lost my mind. I still refer to this as my pale-yellow towel miracle. We were having so much fun in class. All we had to do was request something, and it would show up.

One of the most powerful synchronicities was when one of the women in the group asked us to pray for her sick dog at home. She was a religious woman and told the class she prayed every night to Mother Mary. I suggested when she prayed to Mother Mary that evening, she might try asking her to heal her dog and if that was the right thing to do. She said she would and she'd let us know. The next week, we were all sitting on pins and needles when she arrived. She went to bed as she did every night, saying a prayer to Mother Mary, asking her to please help her dog. She asked her to heal the dog or let it pass away comfortably. As she was drifting off to sleep, she suddenly felt a presence in her bedroom. She said she sat up and saw Mother Mary take off her blue mantilla, place it over the dog, and disappear. Her beloved dog passed away that night as he slept. No one could speak; it was such a beautiful story.

In all of "The Artist's Way" classes I taught that followed, everyone had stories of the synchronistic miracles that showed up in their lives. It was amazing. The question then became: Is there really someone or something out there listening to us? Do we live in an intelligent and responsive universe? As I reflect on those first experiences, I smile for their encouraging us to continue our journeys and learn a new way of being, thinking, acting, and seeing. Over the years, I have learned we cannot force a synchronicity, nor can we expect to find one on command. They arrive in the moment, and if we are not paying attention, we will miss them. They are gifts from the universe, and all we must do is pay attention. What I do know for sure is synchronicities happen every day for each one of us. If you are conscious of the moment and awake to the magic of the world around you, you will start experiencing them all the time. Listen, the universe is whispering. Let the adventure begin.

WHAT I LEARNED BY TEACHING THESE CLASSES

I had been teaching classes based on Julia Cameron's book for a while. There are two homework assignments in the book. One of the assignments is to write your morning pages every day in a stream-of-consciousness approach to writing—a sort of brain drain—without checking spelling or grammar. Imagine my surprise one morning at work when I wrote the following:

> *"There are so many hurting people in the world. All trying to tap their way out of a shell and emerge healthy. So many barriers. Look to do this work joyfully. Don't be your own worst friend. Remember, you are doing the best you can with the tools you have. Allow this process to go on and get out of the way, especially if you are not serving yourself. Always remember you are not alone. There are many entities around who are assisting people in their growth toward the light. They may not be aware of it at first, but the moments of synchronicity are too numerous for the unfolding conscious mind to ignore. It is truly wonderful to observe all the positive growth through pain and the emergence of a new*

spiritual being that will shed light on people in their own way. One must experience the pain and anguish in order to see it is only a momentary stop-off in life before they get on to the real work of living. There is a plan for everyone, and everyone must take the journey alone."

After writing this down, I was in utter dismay as I would have never used some of the words I had written here. I read it over and over again, and I knew it wasn't me doing this writing. But then who was it? I couldn't wait to tell anybody who would listen. I showed it to my husband, children, and friends. They thought it was great, but like me, they had absolutely no idea what it really meant.

But in the heavens, another dialogue was happening. These words ignited a team of guides who began my healing process. I was told on the page it needed to happen. My guides got to work and they never gave up, and neither did I. I showed up, and I did the work. I learned through my experiences and started teaching as I began to heal. I had to learn how to come from a place of love by opening my heart, letting go of judgment and fear, and being in empathy and compassion for myself and others in our individual soul journeys. I had to learn how to let go and not be in control. I learned the only thing I could control was my attitude. This was a hard one to let go. Learning to become sincerely grateful and experiencing this gave me an incredible feeling that is hard to explain. It's a feeling that washes all over you when you're in the humble state of gratitude. On this journey of self-healing,

I also came to understand I wasn't alone and there was somebody or something with me all the time, prodding me, teaching me, and sometimes even yelling at me. When I learned about my guardian angel and when we die—we really don't die, only our bodies die—that gave me a lot of comfort.

I can honestly say this journey has brought me to a place in my life where I feel such love and gratitude for all the beings seen and unseen that have molded me and helped me along this path. I have come to feel the love flowing to and from my heart, giving me a profound respect for everyone's life journey. We are all souls coming to earth for a purpose. The second great gift gleaned from The Artist's Way was to have a play date, a time to nurture the child within you. Ever since taking on the practice of 'morning pages' and having 'play dates' with the child within me, my own self-healing path has assisted in my work with others.

AND THE HEALING CONTINUES

After teaching The Artist's Way for a long time, I decided to teach others what I was learning on my spiritual quest. I love planting seeds, and I also loved working with groups. So, I decided to start a new group in my home called *Caterpillars to Butterflies*. My intention was to continue to explore and acquire new knowledge and awareness about how our thoughts become reality.

My very first women's spiritual group met at 7:00 p.m. in my home. My friend assisted me in setting up the space in my living room. As I loved playing, I decided to invite my grandmother and mother to the very first women's spirituality group meeting. I filled my grandmother's crystal bowl with white sand, a sprig of sage, and a small clay goddess. While filling the bowl, I said out loud, "Grandma, I am formally inviting you to the first women's spirituality group meeting." Then I took my mother's beautiful crystal vase and filled it with bright gladiolus, her favorite flowers, and said, "Mom, I am formally inviting you to my first women's spirituality group meeting." My friend said, "Lynn, your aunt wants to be invited, too." This statement took me by surprise. My grandmother, mother, and aunt had all passed away, but I just thought it would be fun to invite them. I was playing. I didn't know they were listening.

Then I said, "Aunt Mildred, I am formally inviting you to the first women's spirituality group, and the Lladro doves on the piano you gave me will be your representation." To my surprise, my friend then said, "Your aunt says they are not in an important enough position and should be moved." It was at that moment I knew my aunt was there, as there was no one, living or dead, who would have uttered those words except my aunt Mildred. So, I moved the Lladro doves closer to a modern piece of sculpture on the piano. I then asked my friend to ask my aunt if they were in the right place now. My friend said, "She says yes." What an incredible way to start my first women's group. My ancestors were listening, giving me another woo woo moment. It was by creating and leading this group I was inspired to continue my spiritual quest. What I learned, I taught.

THE LESSONS FROM MY HEART

As a social worker, I worked with many families going through challenging times in their lives. As an empath, I could feel their sadness and anger, and I brought these feelings home with me. Obviously, this was not a good thing to hold in my heart. So, I was led to a workshop put on by a shaman. The only thing I remember from this workshop was the group was given clay to make into something. At first, I didn't know what I was going to make but I decided on a heart-shaped vase for a flower. Sweet. But I knew it wasn't complete and kept working on it until I had removed the bottom piece of clay, and now it wasn't a cute heart vase anymore. Instead, it was a heart that let water or whatever you put into it flow out the bottom of the heart. At first, I didn't get the message being presented to me, but the longer I looked at it, the more it made sense. I was not to hold other's emotions in my heart but to let their worries, sadness, hurts, angers flow in and out of my heart. I didn't know this at the time, but being an empath is sometimes wonderful, but if the heart holds it all, it will cause trouble. At the end of the workshop, we all placed our art pieces in a sacred fire transmuting them.

BODY FOCUSING: ANOTHER MESSAGE FROM MY HEART

A numerologist I met recommended I learn about 'body focusing,' so I signed up for it as I was ready for a new adventure. Body focusing is a technique used to receive and confirm one's own 'inner intelligence.' When we listen to our bodies, they provide us a wealth of knowledge. Who knew? As the instructor explained the technique, we were paired up for the experience.

One individual would sit quietly, focusing internally, while the other would sit next to the person to reiterate whatever the person verbalized. In taking notice of whatever pain, twinge, or feeling arises within the other person's body, the person focusing could also ask whether her own body has anything to say. If it does, then the person should allow that part of the body to speak of it. If it doesn't, then that part of the body does not feel safe. Focusing is a great way to listen to the body and its source of wisdom for your growth and self-inquiry. Your body talks to you, and often it says something you may not want to hear.

I sat opposite my partner, and going into a brief meditation, I asked my body what it wanted to say. The body answered immediately when my ears started to buzz. I said, "My ears want to speak." My partner then repeated, "Your ears would like to speak." "Yes," I said. The next thing you're supposed to do is say hello to whatever is arising for attention. Addressing whatever arises is important, as it marks the beginning of the inner relationship between you and your inner body intelligence. I asked my ears if they had anything they wanted to say and received an immediate "Yes." The next thing my ears said was, "We are tired of listening." My partner repeated what I said, and then I really got nervous. That message scared me, as all I did on my job was listen to the parents, the children, and all of the other professions invested in whatever social-work case I was overseeing. As part of the process, I asked my ears to say anything else to me. I held my breath for the answer. My ears gave me another message, and I spoke it out loud. "My ears are saying I should listen from my heart." My partner reiterated what they had communicated. I was at a loss. On the one hand, I understood the message, but on the other hand, I didn't have the foggiest idea how to listen from my heart. It would take a while to download and I was surprised by the powerful information my body communicated to me in the first class.

I signed up for another focusing class immediately, as this one had been so powerful. I had to learn how to listen from my heart and not just my ears. This turned out to be yet another gift.

Part of my job as a child welfare social worker is being able to be present. It's called being a silent witness. Since I'm normally a very chatty person, I needed help and practice to become a 'silent witness.'

I knew it was necessary to simply listen and refrain from speaking. I was a 'fixer.' I have always had an opinion or a solution, even if no one wanted to hear about it. But now, I had to learn to just listen. Observation is a powerful tool. When silently listening to what is being communicated, the body language also tells a story. So, my desire to be a better listener was an important goal.

At my second body-focusing class, I was paired with three women I didn't know. As we began the process, the first woman to focus had a remarkable experience. What rose to her attention was a discomfort in her uterus. She said, "My uterus is painful." The group then said back to her, "Your uterus wants your attention, and it says it's painful." "Yes," she responded. She went on to tell us her uterus was saying it was unhappy because she had not had children. Then she said, "An angel is telling me that I have a lot of creativity to be birthed." Her uterus, she said, "felt joy." At the end of her focusing time, she was in tears, and so were we. That was so powerful.

It was then my turn. I was so excited thinking about how an angel had come to her. Quietly I sat on the floor with my legs crossed in a yoga position. My eyes were tightly shut, and I could feel my breathing as I waited for some form of communication from my body. Then it started, I began to feel very heavy and large; I felt huge. As I continued to tell the partners what was happening, I started to bend forward, saying I felt larger and larger. My shoulders and head began to bend over my legs. I kept feeling very heavy and dark. I felt like a massive, large, brown boulder. I even had green moss on me. "Oh, my goodness," I said, "I am a rock. I am a very large brown rock with moss on me. I am not even a cute rock."

I had no idea what was happening to me, and then I began to see horses, wagons, people, and towns materialize in front of me. I could see the blue and cloudy sky above me and the hard, dirt ground and knew how difficult it was for the travelers in the early days of settling the town. I had become the silent witness. I was a boulder and could only observe, not say a word unless you understood rock talk. I was flabbergasted. What an incredible way to show someone like me exactly what a silent witness experienced. The experience of being the silent witness was perfect. I was told to listen from my heart and just be present for another's journey. The new task was to learn how to integrate the experience and then teach others. This wasn't an easy assignment, but I kept on trying and gained a softer me who eventually learned how to listen. My clients felt heard and not judged. It is an incredible feeling when you realize your requests are not only being heard but answered in such a surprising fashion.

I discovered we need to learn to trust what is in our hearts and forgive the past that has caused us pain. Then, when we see these events as our teachers, our hearts can open, and we can choose to love.

DO YOU BELIEVE IN ANGELS?

In my job, I occasionally had to remove children from their home or school. This was very scary for the children, and I always asked them, "Do you believe in angels?" Whatever they answered, we would talk about their special guardian angel. This was comforting for them. I told them they each had a very special guardian angel who came with them when they were born and would comfort and protect them throughout their lives. They could even talk to their angel.

HOW I FOUND OUT ABOUT GUARDIAN ANGELS

Growing up, I didn't know about angels. My family never talked about them, and I didn't know Jewish people even had angels. After researching, I learned Jewish people believe angels are supernatural beings and appear widely throughout Jewish literature. For example, in the Torah, an angel prevents Abraham from slaughtering his son Isaac, appears to

Moses in the burning bush, and gives direction to the Israelites during the desert sojourn following the liberation from Egypt. In later biblical texts, angels are associated with visions and prophecies and are given proper names. Well, that was certainly interesting, and now my encounters with angels made sense to me.

One summer morning, as I sat outside writing, I looked up at my kitchen window and experienced a goose-bump moment. In the kitchen window was a large profile of an angel with wings. I looked at trees, I looked at anything that could produce this visualization but found nothing. I had never seen anything like this in my whole life. I stood there with my mouth open. While this experience was incredible, I felt confused and didn't know what to make of it. I watched for a long time, and it never left and never said anything to me. I eventually went back into the house.

My next encounter with guardian angels came a few months later. I am not usually depressed, but this morning as I was going to a home visit, I was depressed, and I was driving a crappy car that only had one working radio station. On this station was a program called "Seeing Beyond." The host had a psychic on her show. The psychic was very interesting, and I was intrigued by the conversation. I knew I had to call this physic and schedule an appointment. I pulled over along the side of the road, wrote down the psychic's phone number, and continued going to the home visit. Immediately after returning to my office, I called her. I don't remember her name, but I remember her telling me she had an opening Sunday afternoon, and I should come to see her as I appeared to be in distress. I booked the appointment. I remember her office was a long way from where I lived, and as I drove there, I was nervous. How did she know I was distressed? This was the second time I met with a psychic. The first time I was sent to one because I was concerned I might be killed on my job. I learned later that one's thoughts create reality, and I had a very dangerous thought in my fear-based brain. This particular visit to the psychic ended with him saying I would not be killed on my job, which relieved a lot of concern.

As I entered, she told me there was someone with me. I looked behind me, and no one was there. She said it again, "There is someone with you." I was flabbergasted; I didn't bring anyone with me. Or so I thought. She said the individual's name began with the letter M. I said, "Mother?" She said, "No." I said, "Michael?" She said, "No, the name begins with an M and a strong R." I didn't have a clue. She reiterated, saying, "An M and a strong R." Still nothing. She then said, "You were named after this person." Oh, my goodness, I was named after my grandfather on my mother's side, and his name was Myer. The psychic said, "Yes, that is the person with you. He is your guardian angel, and he is depressed." I said, "What is he depressed about?" I don't remember anything else about my hour session with her, but I did learn my guardian angel was my grandfather. That was thrilling.

MARY'S GUARDIAN ANGEL

On a cold, wintery morning, I received a telephone call from a teacher telling me Mary, a second-grader, and a little girl on my caseload had arrived that morning dressed in shorts, a tee-shirt, jellies, and no jacket. I had been involved in this case because the mother had a drinking problem and was in an outpatient treatment program at this time. I didn't know her mother had relapsed and had sent her seven-year-old to school dressed for summer. I picked Mary up and told her we were going shopping for some new warm clothes, that we'd have lunch, and maybe go to the movies. Mary was excited.

In the car ride to Target, I asked Mary if she believed in angels. She said, without any trepidation, "Yes, my grandfather is my guardian angel." She continued, "I met him before I was born, and he told me he would always love and take good care of me." "That is fantastic," I said. "Let's invite your grandfather to go with us today." And we did. Mary, her guardian angel, and I went to Target, bought some warm clothes, and then headed off to McDonald's for lunch, and afterward, a movie. We both had a remarkable day.

After the movie, I phoned her grandmother and explained the circumstances; I asked if I could place Mary with her until I investigated the matter. The grandmother was thrilled to have Mary stay with her. We drove up to her apartment just as she was getting home from work. I mentioned to the grandmother the conversation I'd had with Mary when she told me about her grandfather being her guardian angel. The grandmother smiled and said that as soon as Mary started talking, she had asked to see her grandfather. When she was told he had passed away, she got hysterical. She told her mother and her grandmother that she met him, and that he couldn't be dead. They took her to where he was buried, and she just sobbed. Her grandmother said Mary told them all about her conversations with him before she was born and told them what he looked like. Her grandmother was astonished at how clear Mary was in her description of him.

WE ARE ALL HERE FOR A PURPOSE

At the end of my session with Hans Christian King, he referred me to a spiritual coach who proved to be a very significant teacher. I started meeting with her once a week, and in the sessions, she used meditation as a tool to awaken my inner guidance. I didn't even know I had inner guidance. But I did.

One of the first experiences with the spiritual teacher came when I spoke to a six-month-old baby who informed me why she was born and what she came here to do.

THE STORY OF JO ANN

I met Jo Ann's parents before she was born. I was called to assess the situation because both of the parents were using drugs. The father was HIV-positive, and the mother was pregnant. I remember clearly the apartment was filled with creepy crawly creatures, the kinds of animals you see in the woods. They had three large boa constrictors, mice to feed them, and a very large iguana. Upon entering and seeing this menagerie of reptiles, I sought a safe place to sit for the interview. From the interview, I learned both parents were wounded children themselves, having come from abusive families, and both had been sexually abused. They were now into many different drugs.

Jo Ann was born soon after this interview.

There were complications with Jo Ann's birth as she needed to be placed in a neonatal unit. When a mother uses drugs, her baby will likely experience withdrawal symptoms. The baby was tiny, had poor feeding habits, seizures, irritability, and high-pitched crying, and had a hard time being comforted. The hospital offered a number of support services and training for the parents on how to interact and care for their baby. Unfortunately, like many addicts, Jo Ann's parents would sleep all day, arriving at the hospital late at night.

They were very annoyed the nurses at night would not tell them how to take care of their daughter. With the care Jo

Ann needed and the parents' lack of responsibility, I needed to place the baby into protective care. The police were called to the hospital, and we let the parents know their little girl was being placed into a medically fragile infant home. They were given the papers and had to appear in court the following Monday for a hearing where the judge sees how the parents have been cooperating with Child Protection Services and how the baby is doing. Jo Ann was thriving in the medical-fragile infant home and doing nicely. Her parents were participating in all the court-ordered services. The mother had gone into an in-patient drug treatment program, which provided her with support, counseling, tools, and lessons on how to take care of her baby when she would be returned to her custody. On the other hand, the father was in an out-patient treatment program and not doing well. He showed an inability to cope with a variety of stresses and mood swings. Although he was testing negative for drug abuse, I just knew he was lying.

At the court hearing, my recommendation was for the child to continue in the medically fragile home, with the parents continuing their individual drug-treatment programs and having individual counseling. The court agreed. As a child advocate, I was concerned the parents would do just enough to get their baby girl back. I was not happy. But it was here where I learned we all have a soul contract, and now I was going to find out what Jo Ann's contract was. This was before I knew how God really operated, how some children have a heavy load upon birth and lessons to be learned as they grew.

Jo Ann was thriving in her medically fragile home, and her parents were more or less cooperating with the court and what they were supposed to do, but I really didn't want to return this child to these parents. I thought she would be much better off in a home where she would be safe and well taken care of, as well as loved. While working on this case, in a session with my therapist, I told her about the child and how I wanted her to be placed in a good loving home. She then asked me a very provocative question. "What does the child want?" I responded, "I don't know, as she is only six months old."

My therapist then asked me if I had ever communicated with another person asking permission to speak from my higher self to his or her higher self. I said I had done so in another counselor's office a long time ago. She said in this session, we would ask permission from Jo Ann's higher self and ask what she wanted to see happen. I went into a relaxed meditative state where I asked Jo Ann's higher self for permission to speak to her from my higher self. The response was, "Yes." The fact was I did not want Jo Ann to be returned to her parents so soon. Though they were cooperating, I knew it had not been a sufficiently long enough period of time to risk placing their child back with them. I wanted her to stay in her medically fragile home longer, for at least another six months.

There I sat and asked a beautiful, little, six-month-old girl what she wanted. I was astounded by her response. Her higher self told me, "I was born to show my parents how to love. This is why I came." I was floored. I had absolutely no idea I could communicate with a six-month-old baby and get such a clear message.

At the next meeting with Jo Ann's father, I told him exactly what had transpired in my therapy session and what Jo Ann said to me. It is strange, but I didn't worry he would go to my supervisor and tell her what a crackpot social worker I was. I just felt the need to tell him. Jo Ann went home at eight months of age. She was born to show her mother and father how to love. Though I still wanted to keep her out longer, the courts placed her back home with her mom and dad. They left California soon after and moved to Oregon. The father wrote me from Oregon to let me know they just had another child, a baby boy born without HIV. I wrote back, telling him I was very happy for their family, and reminded him of what Jo Ann had said about being born to show them how to love.

YAY! I FINALLY GOT TO MEET MY GUIDE

I met my guide when I was working with my spiritual therapist. One afternoon, as our session ended, she told me my guide wanted to communicate with me. I was astonished as I didn't know anything about guides at this time. She told me everyone is born with a guide, but we don't remember. She continued. I was to sit in a comfortable spot with a pad of paper and a pen. I was to ask what my guide wanted to say to me and to make little circles until I received the communication. I had experienced automatic writing once before, but I never gave it a second thought.

The next morning, I sat down with a pad of paper and wrote, "What do you wish to tell me?" Suddenly, after I began making the little circles, I started receiving a message from an inner source. I heard it inside my head. The message started by saying, "I have been waiting a very long time to finally connect with you."

This meeting with my guide (whom I later learned was Aaron) became an inner source of guidance, support, and love. Whenever I hit the proverbial rabbit hole, he would guide me out of it and provide new insights. In the beginning, I wrote to Aaron almost every day. I would just allow the flow of words to pass through me onto the pages. When I would get worried or scared, I would write. His message was always the same: *Don't worry, you will be given clear direction if you pay attention. We are here for you, and you are needed.*

I learned guides are special gifts. Everyone born has a guide or two. Some people call them angels, or higher selves, or spirit guides. Their job is one of loving, guiding, educating, and supporting you. They appear when called upon in prayer or exasperation or as an inner knowing. They will never interfere with a person's journey unless asked, or it is a life-or-death situation.

Once you step onto the path of 'awakening,' your guides take a more active role in your life. Synchronistic events happen, teachers appear, and the perfect song or poem appears to give you the exact encouragement you need to continue.

I was very slow to awaken to the path of 'awakening.' My guide Aaron told me he had been trying to connect with me many times before I finally slowed down enough to hear him.

Here is how he tried connecting with me. (I am surprised he didn't quit.)

The first memory of something seeming very strange to me was very late one Saturday night. My husband and I had just returned home from an evening out. Getting ready for bed, I heard some beautiful violin music. I was not a musician, but I knew somehow this was a concerto. I had never heard of a concerto and really didn't have a clue what one was. I just knew inside it was called a concerto. The beautiful melody played repeatedly. My husband didn't hear it. After fifteen minutes of listening to this beautiful song, I fell asleep.

The next incident happened one evening while sitting on a sofa. I looked out the window, and in the bushes in my yard, I saw what appeared to be a velvet painting of a beautiful young girl with red lips and black hair. That evening I asked everyone who came over to sit in the same seat I sat in to see the picture. I was disappointed no one saw this beautiful painting of the lady except me.

In my third experience, someone was trying to contact me while washing the dishes. I was washing away when I heard what appeared to be Morse code, "dot dot, dash dash." I laughed out loud and said, "Whomever you are trying to contact me, I don't know music, I can't paint, and I have no idea what is being said to me in Morse code." When I said these words, the Morse code abruptly stopped. I laughed and thought this experience was funny and never gave it much thought until I finally connected with my guide.

In recalling other strange occurrences, I think the second time someone tried to contact me was my experience with the Russian doctor, who I sat in front of with one eye open and the other shut. I was skeptical and judgmental. It was here I was told to, "shut up and close my eyes." Aaron told me later he was the one who said, "Lynn, shut your eyes and be still." At the time, it never dawned on me I had a guide speaking to me.

The fourth time I was contacted was incredibly fun—it literally blew my socks off as I received a channeled message one morning while writing my morning pages at work. This message gave me my directions. I was to heal first so I could assist others in their process. At the time, I thought it was wonderful to receive this message but I had no idea it came from my guide. I really am slow at receiving messages, but I figure it out eventually.

WELCOME LYNN, YOU FINALLY GOT IT

And I finally got it when my spiritual therapist said to me, "Lynn, your guide has been wanting to communicate with you, and this is how you do it." With this prompting, I finally sat myself down with a pen and a piece of white paper. Not knowing what to expect, I listened, and I heard, and I wrote down what was said, which was: "I have been waiting a long time to begin this communication with you." It was a defining moment in my life, and this connection with my guidance team completely altered the course of my life.

I received my assignment, I had to heal first so I could assist others, and thus the path of self-healing began. I am always shown where to go next, and I trust the guidance even if I wasn't aware I was being guided.

It is miraculous to experience an awakening, where so much guidance is being shared all of the time. I am in awe of how wonderful, loving, and funny one's guides can be. Never in a million years could I have done any of this without them. There are no words for how grateful I feel and how much love I have for them. It is impossible to fully express what you will feel when you open your heart and mind to ask your guides for assistance. It is an immeasurable joy.

To connect with your spirit guide, angels, or your personal guardian angel, first and foremost, you must ask. There are many ways to connect, and no method is better than the other. Some people choose to meditate, others prefer to communicate through their dreams, and others still can simply talk to their guides. In my case, I wrote down what I was being told. Revelations can come in moments of reflection while sitting, daydreaming, walking, or in the shower. These revelations give insights. Learn how to trust the thoughts you receive.

Remember, your guide or angel will always love, encourage, support, and teach you. Whenever I was faced with a difficult situation or feeling, I knew I could contact my guide Aaron and get the needed assistance, direction, and support. I could always ask for help and input, and I still do.

The wisdom and the humor were always perfect. As I started making the small changes, becoming more aware and conscious of my old patterns and beliefs, I was always rewarded with new insights. I saw with fresh eyes, as well as an open heart. In my healing process, I traced many of my core issues, patterns, and beliefs back to my childhood experiences. I let my child within know whatever was said or done to hurt her was not true. She is worthy, she is enough, and she has come here for a reason.

As I was writing this piece, I stopped and asked my guide, Aaron, to explain it better than I can. He said, "Everyone born has a guide who takes birth with them. The guide is assigned to assist the soul in awakening and allowing new information to be downloaded into the brain and body. This is needed to assist in changing the frequency on Earth from negative to positive, from hatred to love. Love is the highest frequency, and with a loving heart, the world changes one by one. The time has arrived that all the guides have been waiting for, a new awakening happening on the planet. Many people are beginning to tune into their guidance. Some call their guidance coming from angels, higher selves, guides, or God. The messages are the same, and all the messages boil down to stepping out of fear and stepping into love."

Every encounter you have in life is for a reason, and there is always a lesson.

MET THE INCREDIBLE SQUIRREL LADY IN THE RAIN

One Sunday morning, I decided to take my dog for a walk in the park near my home. It was overcast with a chance of rain, but my pup loved going to the park, and I loved making her happy. That Sunday would turn out to lead to an important meeting for me.

As we walked in the park, I noticed an older woman colorfully dressed, holding a bag of whole peanuts and going from tree to tree, placing the nuts on the ground for the squirrels. She waited until a squirrel would come down the tree and grab a peanut and scurry back up. My dog in her younger years was known as a squirrel hunter, but she was now older and ignored them.

It started to rain, and I walked over to the woman and asked her if I could walk beside her and share my umbrella. She said, "Yes, that would be nice." And that is how this yet another new adventure began.

As we walked under the umbrella, she started telling me all about herself. She launched into how all the life experiences we have are meant to teach us. Therefore, it is important to pay attention to what comes into your life. You meet up with all the people and experiences your soul needs for your highest good. And hopefully, you grow since our purpose in this world is to grow into loving human beings. She told me how thoughts create our reality, and on and on. It was as if I was in a spiritual classroom. This was a significant "kahuna" synchronicity.

I was mesmerized by her stories and the love that flowed from her. The squirrels were happy and fed, and as she left to go home, she invited me to come to her church the following Sunday where she plays the organ every Sunday morning. She added that the leader of the church communicated with deceased loved ones. I asked her if he was a medium, and she said, "Yes." I was intrigued since I had never met a medium. I said I would be there.

Of course, I did not want to go alone as that would be too scary, so I asked one of my friends to accompany me on this adventure. We arrived at the church the following Sunday and took seats in the middle of the room. The squirrel lady was playing the organ, and she smiled at me.

The service was comprised of inspirational teachings, meditation, singing, and a psychic demonstration. Toward the end of the service, church members passed out pieces of white paper and pens. The leader said people who wanted to ask a question from someone who had departed could write it down and he would pick a few questions to answer. Oh boy, now it's going to get good. I wrote my question, not directed toward any one person, almost immediately. I asked, "Why did you send me here?" I folded the paper and placed it in the basket being circulated. When he received the basket, the leader took out one folded piece of paper, placed it on his forehead, and then answered the question. As I sat quietly focused, I silently asked that he read my question. To my delight and fear, he reached in and pulled out my question. He placed it on his forehead and said, "Your mother sent you here today as there was a message in the sermon that she wanted you to hear."

I almost fell out of my seat as I couldn't remember anything about the sermon. He asked who in the audience had asked the question. I answered, and he asked me to stand up and explain what I learned in the sermon. I went blank. "I do not remember hearing a message for me," I said. (In retrospect, I remembered when I listened to the service, something stood out and got my attention but standing there, I just went blank.) It was embarrassing, to put it mildly. I was nervous; first, my mother was talking to me, and she had passed away a long time ago, and then I thought maybe the leader could read my mind. I stood there until he said, "Your mother wanted you to hear the part about love being the most powerful emotion and to open your heart more. That is why you are here." I did remember the part about love in the sermon.

I never went to that church again, and I never saw the squirrel lady. She was a gift. The beginning of new adventures that opened my heart even more. I knew this was a significant message and was thrilled my mom had sent it.

THE POWER OF NEGATIVE THOUGHTS

I never knew thoughts were as powerful as they are. I have asked many people this question: "Do you know your thoughts can create your reality?" And everyone says, "Yes." But I don't think they have any idea how powerful this can be because our thoughts are built on our unconscious beliefs. So, it was time for me to learn another lesson.

When I began my career as a child abuse social worker, I must admit the thought that I could be killed on my job entered my head. Although it was scary, it didn't stop me. I wanted to make a difference in the world, and I wanted to do it with families and children.

At the time, I didn't understand thoughts were energy and negative thoughts were not good. Now, I know you can manifest fears into your reality but it's not a good idea to put fear out into the universe.

However, my guide, knowing what my thoughts could eventually produce, steered me to a synchronistic encounter with a pediatric oncologist who was on her way to a walk-about with the Navajos. My husband was attending a class in Scottsdale, Arizona and I went along. I ended up sitting next to a woman, clearly a move set up by my guide. The woman said she was a pediatric oncologist who didn't like children. I laughed out loud, telling her I worked for Family & Children Services and was a strong child advocate. We both laughed and ordered a drink. I didn't know it at the time, but this airplane encounter would become vital for me.

The conversation was extremely interesting. She told me about her childhood and how her old home had a ghost living there. She said the ghost was not scary, and she told me all about her spiritual quests. Being such a newbie on the path, I was enthralled by all her experiences. She was on her way to walk in the Grand Canyon with the Navajos. At the end of the plane ride, she told me I was supposed to go to Sedona as I needed to do something there. As we disembarked, I knew sitting next to her was not an accident, and I was bubbling with excitement. We hugged, and I felt a deep awareness she had been a part of my learning. I told her, "I was meant to meet you." She agreed. It was our destiny to meet. She helped me see how to take away my fear because my guide knew how my fears manifest. I couldn't wait to tell my husband about what she told me.

My husband and I rented a car, and the next day after his class, we drove to Sedona. I had no idea what I was looking for. We stopped at an information booth, I told the woman my story, and she sent us to a psychic bookstore. God love my husband, as he was supportive and patient. I looked at all the books, but none of them fell off the shelf. What was I supposed to do? Then I saw a sign the psychic would be back in half an hour. I thought I would give it a whirl. I signed up for a reading. Thirty minutes passed. Then a man, looking like he could be a psychic, came in and sat down. I sat for my session, which was at least thirty minutes. The tape I brought home was blank, and I can only remember one thing from the session. I asked him, "Will I be killed on the job?" His reply was, "No, you will not be killed on the job." He told me other things, but honestly, I don't remember anything except that I was not going to die on the job. I felt very relieved, and we drove back to Scottsdale.

HOW I CREATED AN "I AM GOING TO BE SUED" EXPERIENCE

After I retired from the Department of Family & Children Services, I became a visitation supervisor. My job involved supervising visits for non-custodial parents and their children. Often it was a war zone with the children in the middle. My job consisted of protecting the children and assisting the parents as best I could.

One of the other visitation supervisors asked me, "Did you take out extra insurance for this supervision work?" My response was, "Why do I need insurance?" She went on to say, "You need insurance because you can be sued and lose everything, including your home. You are working with some angry clients, and they can and will sue you."

This was definitely not what I wanted to hear, and this information put me into a tailspin. I never considered my clients could sue me. I worked hard to provide a warm and loving atmosphere for both the parents and the children. The story ahead is how negative thoughts manifest.

I needed insurance, so I contacted the National Association of Social Workers to purchase insurance.

NOW YOU SEE HOW A NEGATIVE THOUGHT MATERIALIZES

One afternoon, a mother asked if I could supervise a visitation between her four children and their father the next day. I responded I was available. I like to go to the house of a new client to meet with the children before the visitation. This way, they get a chance to meet me and ask any questions they may have about the visit and my supervisory role.

The day before the visit, I drove to the house to meet with the children. What I encountered was not what I expected.

In the driveway stood a man who looked like a guard with a gun tucked in his belt. I had been a social worker for a long time, but I had never experienced someone guarding a home. I should have listened to my intuition, but I didn't, and I knocked at the door. The mother answered, interviewed me, and informed me how horrible her former husband was. She then introduced me to her four children. The children basically ignored me and had no questions, so I left.

The next day, I picked up the children and went to the park to meet their father. The children seemed to enjoy the visit, and all went well until I returned the children home. I told the mother it was a good visit. In retrospect, it was clearly not the right thing to say to her as she got furious at me and called me all sorts of names. But this is not the point of the story. What is so important here is that I had previously birthed the fear I could be sued.

I forgot my thoughts are energetic and call to me what I send out. Big mistake. We all create manifestations through thoughts, words, and actions that use energy to form objects, conditions, and experiences. We are bringing energy to everything we do, think, or say. Therefore, my fearful thought was alive and well and in the process of manifesting. I didn't know it at the time, but I would have a big surprise Monday morning.

On Monday morning, my office phone had a message from an attorney. The attorney stated he represented Mrs.

Blank and to call him back. Mrs. Blank was the woman whose children I had just supervised, and she was not happy with me.

Immediately, I shifted into fear mode. I Googled this attorney's name. He was neither a divorce attorney nor a family attorney. He was a personal attorney, and my thoughts went to, "This client is going to sue me!" Before I even took a breath, I immediately called one of my friends who is an attorney. I explained the circumstances, and she reassured me there was no way this person could sue me. I responded that people sue each other all the time, even when facts don't support it. She agreed, but there was no comfort in that.

I never returned the attorney's call, but I learned how fast I could manifest my fear. I quickly engaged in changing my thought processes. In learning from these lessons, I shared with others the importance of how our thoughts can create our reality. What a great lesson! I don't wish to repeat it again.

One of the questions I've been asked over and over again is, "How do you know that your thoughts can create your reality?"

At the beginning of this journey, I can honestly say I had no idea I was creating my own reality. It never occurred to me to pay attention to my thoughts. As a young woman, I went through life unaware that my thoughts were creating my experiences. Then there was the Ah-Ha moment and a shift, and I got to see just how my thoughts were creating everything.

When we are born, we are little love bugs, and then we get downloaded just like computer software, or an app. Our thoughts are downloaded from our parents, belief system, culture and values, religion, and early life experiences. Children get their thoughts from their parents and so forth and so on. These thoughts and beliefs are continuously operating in the background of our unconscious mind.

They come out when we are negative or when we are in a new situation. For example, negative thoughts such as, "I can't do this, I have never been in a good relationship, I am never going to get it, be successful, lose weight, find love, etc., etc." These thoughts are thrown out into the universe whenever we decide or enter new relationships. Once we acknowledge how powerful our thoughts are, then at a conscious level, we can create what we desire instead of being subject to the effect of unconscious behavior. You are the creator. Thoughts are energy, and we are attracting to us what we ask for. I wish I had known this at a younger age. I could have saved myself many tears. But then, what would I have learned?

This recognition along my journey became enlightening in the most beautiful way. With my unconscious ignorance, especially relating to painful emotional experiences, I never realized their significance as lessons arriving in my life based on my own thoughts, whether consciously or unconsciously created. Observing these recollections as lessons in my youth has helped me assist others to reflect on how childhood memories and thoughts are very much a part of creating one's future. Once people can see the power of what is operating, they can shift their thinking and become a more conscious creator instead of an unconscious one.

Traveling down this spiritual path, I quickly learned that my thoughts, whether positive or negative, were creating my reality, a fact I continue to observe, teach, and absorb to this day.

HERE COMES THE EMOTION CALLED ANGER

Since I started on this path of healing, my intentions have been to be a conduit of more light and love. I was doing well until my guides decided to hit me with one of my big challenging personality traits—my anger.

My anger was preventing my heart from opening to its full expression. I knew my lessons were being presented to me in increments by my team of guides, angels, ancestors, and master teachers. These teachers pushed me, cajoled, and lovingly presented me with challenges to support my desire to start living from a heart filled with love and light.

In the summer of 2002, I met a woman healer who studied with the renowned healer from Brazil, John of God. At our sessions, she asked the group a question, and then your individual question would be answered by her reading your energy as she answered your question.

My question was simply, where do I go next? It was always my go-to question. Often, I was frustrated my life dreams were not coming to fruition in the timely manner I desired. I knew on some level I had to go back to surrender faith and divine timing, which is what I expected to hear. I was surprised when she informed me I would now be working on my anger. She said my anger was stopping my heart from healing. Anger was a barrier to my intention. She told me to purchase holly drops and place them in water, and whenever I became angry, to drink the holly water. This was not a pun or a joke; it was holly water, not holy water. Now, ask me if I immediately went out and purchased these holly drops; the answer is no. I told you I am a slow learner.

Anger is the very first emotion that comes up when I am fearful, sad, hurt, rebuffed, or injured. It has been a strong cloak of support to my inner sensitivity. When do you start leaving an emotion behind? So, I thought about it for the next couple of months. I even wrote to my guide Aaron, and he suggested I pay attention to how it arose in my life. I didn't have to act on it but acknowledge it as it is telling me something.

I learned my support team doesn't present a subject for your review just once; my lessons were repeated until I got them. As I healed my conditioned layers by paying attention and being conscious, I observed my anger and learned not to express it as it was no longer needed, nor did it serve my intentions.

My guru, Sai Maa, offered this incredible message which rang loud and clear. "Remember, at any moment you can leave the planet. Every moment is precious, so do the work and zoom ahead."

Sai Maa was choosing to create masters for mastery. She stated it was vital we stop being emotional as we needed to stop judging others. Watch your words and actions as they are essential. The same message was coming to me as my brain screamed, I like anger; anger was comfortable. But now, I would have to be responsible with my thoughts. I am a work-in-progress.

Where did this anger start? I used to say when you have a strong emotion or feeling, see if you can sit with it with interested curiosity and feel it in your presence, in your body, to find out if you can trace it on a timeline in your life. Emotions are important because they tell you where and how you've been injured. I needed to practice what I preached. You have heard the saying, "You teach what you need to learn." I started my trip down memory lane with my support team. I was conscious of their presence, love, and encouragement on the journey of seeing and letting go of an emotion that no longer served me or my worldview. My anger came from my childhood when I didn't know how to handle situations, so I would just get angry. As I became aware of my anger as one of my character traits, I learned to be much more conscious when it shows up.

ANOTHER LESSON: MIRRORING

This lesson is fun once you recognize it. At first, I didn't have a clue, and it took me a while to really get it. It all started at a women's workshop on self-esteem. I didn't have much and, again, felt even more "less than" as I looked around the room. I remember clearly saying to a woman in the group, "You are the kindest and nicest woman." I thought it was a great compliment and thought she would just say, "Thank you." Instead, she said, "I am just mirroring you." What? I repeated the compliment, unsure she heard me, and she repeated, "I am just mirroring you." I so did not get it.

Now, I get it! I learned what you like about another, you like about yourself, and what you don't like about another, you don't like about yourself. Whoa! This was an entirely new concept for me. I can now understand how it is an essential lesson for us to come to grips with. Some of our shadow signs are anger, blame, laziness, meanness, judgment, and entitlement. I always smile when someone tells me she doesn't like this person or that person, and she has the same quality but doesn't see it. It's a gift to see the part of ourselves we think no one else sees.

Working on my emotions, especially anger, was an emotional leap for me. I am now looking at my life and the conditions surrounding me with a new sense of grace and detachment. During my life dramas, I can now, for the most part, stand in the very center and see what is being presented and not be attached. It doesn't mean I'm not a little wobbly at times, but is it a new foundation. And it feels really great.

HOW I SAW MY SHADOW SIDE

I love seeing my reflection in other people, especially when they are kind, good, and loving. This always feels positive, but it was difficult for me to see the other part of me that would show up with people who were doing things I didn't like. Never in a million years did I think it had anything to do with me. What I discovered was unless I faced my shadow side, I would continue to see it in others. The world outside of me is only a reflection of the world inside me.

"Nothing ever goes away until it teaches us what we need to know."
~ Pema Chödrön

I have always loved my brother and still do but there were times in both our lives where we would say the same unkind things about each other. He even sold my diary to my boyfriend. That tells you a lot about our relationship.

One summer I was visiting my brother in Chicago and he was in rare form. By rare form I mean he was not kind to his wife, he was judgmental of others, and he was really being a brat. I, of course, was Polly Pure, even if I probably egged him on. I was the older sister.

In all fairness I must admit my brother has one of the kindest hearts in the world. He will do anything for anybody, but this is not what he was showing me that summer. It was the side of him I absolutely detested. Never once did I realize he was mirroring my ugly side.

I went back to San Francisco thinking he will never change. One morning in a jazzercise class, someone asked me a question. My response was very sharp and abrupt. Sharp and abrupt was always something I hated about my brother. Suddenly, a light went on. He is mirroring me, and I don't like what I am seeing. I went back and apologized to the woman for being sharp and abrupt and answered her question. I think I spent the rest of the day dissecting everything I did not like about my brother and seeing how I reflected the same qualities. I could be very sharp and abrupt, I could be mean at times, and I could talk to my husband in an unpleasant manner. Oh ****. That was a big message; I wasn't Polly Pure anymore. I had a shadow side I didn't want anyone to see even when I let it out.

What a lesson. By awakening to the shadow parts of myself I now had a choice. I learned what behaviors no longer served me. I learned I could be unaware of my shadow side when I was busy judging others.

I look at my brother now, warts and all and I know I have the same warts. I love my brother, warts and all. We are closer and have a big heart connection. Thanks, bro; you taught me a big lesson.

> ***"The greatest good you can do for another, is not to share your riches with him, but to reveal to him his own"***
>
> **~ Benjamin Disraeli**

A VERY IMPORTANT LESSON: LEARNING TO STAY BALANCED

One of the most valuable lessons I learned on the healing path was from my teacher Michael Park whose work is based on Gurdjieff's teaching, commonly known as the "The Fourth Way."

He taught staying balanced and being in the moment. The lesson was, you go to your car one morning and notice it has a flat tire. Your son or daughter took it out the night before and never bothered to tell you the tire was flat. However, this morning you have an important meeting and must be there at a specific time. How would you react in this situation?

I learned the moment you lose your balance, your emotions take over, and you lose your reasoning ability. If you stay in the moment, you automatically become balanced and will come up with a plan based on what is, not what ought to be. For example, you can take a cab, call AAA and then the office and let colleagues know you will be delayed. But if you're not in balance, you will get frustrated, angry, and the rest of your day will be thrown off. When you are in the moment, you can see clearly and respond appropriately.

A valuable lesson, particularly whenever you are going into a difficult situation. I taught all my clients who were going through a divorce to place a rock in their pocket and hold onto it when necessary, when emotions ran high. This would help them stay in balance and not succumb to all sorts of emotions.

As a social worker, I went to court every six months and when I became a visitation supervisor, I was continually on the hot seat. The rock was always in my pocket to keep me balanced. This has been one of the best tools I've ever shared with people going through trying times.

The next lesson I learned in the "Fourth Way" was to ask myself what was real in every situation. People always focus on what should be or what could be, but it is important to look at what is showing up. What is real is what is showing up and how we handle the situation. For example, when I was a social worker, we would sit around the conference table every Thursday morning bitching about conditions and policies we had absolutely no control over. What was real were these conditions and policies in place. It was a waste of valuable time trying to change them because we had no power.

Aaron told me in January 1998, "Lynn, stress costs a lot more damage than you know, so when it arises, look and see what it is all about. What can or can't you do about it? Don't get caught in the dance; it's not productive. Stress is an outside source that has inside damage."

I BLEW MY LAST CPS CASE TO GOD.

One of the most challenging cases of my career the year I retired from my job as a child welfare social worker, involved four children—three girls and a boy. The mother was not mentally stable, and the father was a security guard who owned a gun. They all lived together in a studio apartment. I have stepped into some really filthy homes as a social worker, but I had never seen one like this. There wasn't one space in the whole studio apartment that you could sit on or stand in. Clothes were piled up in the bathtub, the counters were filthy, and cockroaches ran up the walls. The children had been ostracized at school because they smelled like urine and were dressed poorly. I had been involved in this case for almost a year and had made some progress, but summer was coming, and these four children were not going to summer school. They would be in the apartment all summer. Therefore, the teachers couldn't report to me.

As I was driving home, I said to myself, I could just leave them there for the summer. But as soon as I had that thought, I knew I couldn't do that, no matter how much work I had to do. As I was driving, I decided to blow the case to God. I opened the window of my car, pretended to put the case in the palm of my hand, and I blew it away. For whatever reason, I felt a sense of relief. I am not a religious person; I just know there is something bigger than I am, operating in the universe.

As I pulled into the garage of my house, I noticed a feather in the passenger seat, and I had no idea how it got there. I laughed. I entered my home, and the phone was ringing. It was a Native American friend. I told her the story and about the feather. She said, "God is telling you to lighten up."

The next morning, I went to work and immediately went into my supervisor's office. I told her about the case and that I blew it to God. She didn't fire me, and that was a good thing. I think she always suspected I was a little strange. I told her I was afraid to pull the four children out of this house because the parents absolutely hate me, and the father has a gun. I asked if I could use the Police Department to assist me. She called the Police Department, and within the hour, I explained why I needed their help. At work, we had family care workers, and they were the ones who were wonderful to work with because they would do all the stuff I couldn't do. The family care worker went to the store and bought backpacks for all four children and filled them with clean clothes, underwear, socks, and a teddy bear.

Now, the only thing we needed was placement. I don't know if any of you know how hard it is to get placement for two children, let alone four children in a family, but I can testify that this never happened during my time working at the Department of Social Services. But I didn't have the case anymore and felt confident a family would take all four siblings. So, I picked up the phone and called the head of placement, who asked me if I was crazy. I said I wasn't and to "call me when you get it." Within a half-hour, he called to say he had found a placement for all four of the children. The home was located forty-five minutes away, and I was so relieved the children would be kept together so they wouldn't be as afraid. The following day the police went to the house to remove the four children. It went smoothly, and the children were brought to the police station, where I met them, and the family care worker, where I explained what was happening. I told them we were going out for lunch at McDonald's, and then we were going to take a ride to see the new house where they were going to stay. The family care worker gave each child a backpack, and after lunch, we drove to the house. I have placed children in homes many times, but this house really stood out. It was on a street with lots of grass, trees, flowers, and kids playing ball in the street. As we entered the house, we could smell the cookies the foster mother had made for the children. She introduced herself and showed the girls their bedroom, which was equipped with three little beds, matching comforters, and a closet filled with clothes and toys. She took the little four-year-old boy and showed him his room. It also had a little bed with a matching comforter, lots of toys, and clothes in the closet.

There also was a very cute little dog that followed them from room to room. It was an overwhelming experience for the children, and I remember the oldest child walking around the kitchen, running her hand on the clean countertop that had nothing on it.

Before I left later in the afternoon, I explained what was going on and explained they would stay in this new home for a while and could phone their parents when they wanted. They didn't pay any attention because they were too busy playing with the dog in the backyard. I gave the foster mother my contact information and all the information I had on the children, including their parents' phone number. I said the children should be allowed to call their parents. We said goodbye to the children and the family, and off we went back to the office. I immediately wrote a court report due the following day. I felt so good. It felt wonderful to have worked this case with something so much bigger than I was, and it couldn't have turned out any better in a million years. I blew the case to God, and God did the work.

Through all the healing work I did on myself, I finally learned the journey of the unfolding process called life had its own rhythm, and the way it was set up was perfect. I was given the message countless times; the only way I could speed up my journey was through surrender. Leaving my controlling self behind was difficult for me, but I watched the miracles happen when I finally learned how to call for assistance.

SAI MAA

In order to tell the story of meeting my guru, Sai Maa Lakshmi Devi, I have to begin with another story about my encounter with another very famous guru called Sathya Sai Baba, an Indian spiritual master. His message for humanity was special, "Love all. Serve All, Help All, Hurt Never." That was a beautiful message. Unfortunately, at the time I encountered Sai Baba, he was no longer living, but that didn't affect my encounters with him, and he showed up twice in my life.

SAI BABA FLASHES ACROSS MY COMPUTER

One Saturday, I invited a friend I met in Egypt who visited the Bay Area to come to my Saturday women's spirituality group. She was a channel for Ascended Masters, and I thought the group would love to witness her channeling. That morning proved to be extremely powerful, and everyone left with new knowledge of what a channeler was as well as the wisdom the Ascended Masters provided.

After the group meeting, my friend and I decided to go out for lunch. As we were walking out the door, I said, "Let's have some fun and invite Sai Baba to join us for lunch." I said this playfully as Sai Baba was reputed to have the ability to bio-locate. Never would I ever have imagined that he heard me. But I was wrong.

Of course, Sai Baba didn't show up at lunch, and I didn't think anything more about the invitation until later in the evening when I was researching another mystic on my computer. All of a sudden, Sai Baba came flashing across my computer screen. There he was with a full head of frizzy hair, a brilliant smile, and wearing his signature orange robe. His appearance took me by surprise, and I remember saying out loud, "Sai Baba can you wait one minute until I finish this work I am doing?" That was the wrong answer. He was not there when I came back. Lesson learned: don't say wait a minute to a guru.

MEETING SAI MAA

A few months after Sai Baba appeared on my computer, my husband and I decided that we wanted to go on an adventure one Saturday afternoon. I read in the paper there was a New Age Expo in San Francisco which sounded interesting. My husband said he would go too, although he wasn't into this "woo woo stuff," as he liked to call it.

He just wanted to keep me company. We drove down to the Expo center in San Francisco, bought our tickets, and standing in the entrance was this beautifully clad Indian woman in a white sari. She looked magnificent; she was singing a song in Hebrew surrounded by some other people also wearing white. Michael and I stopped to listen. There was something so calming and loving being in her presence. And then, out of nowhere, someone yelled, "Why don't you sing a Palestinian song?" She looked him in the eyes and said, "Every song I sing in any language is a song to God." We listened awhile longer and then went to hear the other presenters. We looked all over for information about the woman who had been singing but didn't find anything until we were ready to leave.

We saw a table set up with two young women clad in white as we were leaving. On the table was a very large picture of the woman who had been singing in the entrance. Her name was Chalanda Sai Maa. I had a lot of questions which they kindly answered. She told us Sai Maa was holding darshan at the Marriott Hotel that evening at 7:00 p.m.

I asked what a darshan was and was informed, "Darshan is an opportunity to sit with a holy person." One of the young women offered that Sai Maa was a devotee of Sai Baba. That clinched it; it was such a clear message. I just knew Sai Baba was sending us a message to attend that evening.

As we walked into the Marriott, there was a large picture of Sai Maa in the lobby. We were immediately met by another individual who took us to the coat closet and were told to take off our shoes before we entered the hall. (Thank goodness I had on matching socks that day.) Both of us had some trepidation as we walked through the doors.

Michael and I then walked into the room and sat down with about seventy-five other people waiting with anticipation to see this guru. Then she was there, standing in the doorway wearing a beautiful pale pink sari and smiling. Pouring out of her eyes and smile flowed the most magnificent love and light I had ever felt. I felt the love throughout my entire body. My eyes welled up with tears which slowly ran down my face.

She walked slowly down the center of the room, smiling at everyone. When she walked up on stage, she sat down on a beautifully clad chair with a small footstool for her feet. She looked regal, and she then proceeded to welcome everybody. I don't remember exactly what she talked about that night, but I remember one of her strongest messages was each of us is born with the seeds of Divine love, light, and wisdom. It does not matter what your life experiences have been; that is not who you are now. I didn't quite understand it then, but after spending several week-long retreats with this holy guru, I finally did understand. What a blessing.

At the end of the program, there was chanting of Hindu songs. Michael and I had never chanted a day in our lives, but we joined in even though I could not speak nor pronounce Hindi. I struggled through it, but oh what fun we had. As we left, I can honestly say we both felt higher than kites.

Walking to our car, we just bubbled over with excitement thinking about what we just witnessed, experienced, and what our friends would think of this encounter. How can you explain feeling completely bathed and renewed in her energy? I said a silent prayer to Sai Baba, thanking him for introducing me to Sai Maa.

A few weeks later, Chalanda Sai Maa was going to be in Palo Alto offering darshan. I immediately invited my friends to go with me to hear her. Once again, she was overflowing with love and kindness. I was hooked.

Soon after, I found out Sai Maa was giving a week-long training in Colorado. I loved being in her presence so much I asked a friend to join me. She agreed, and off we went like two teenage girls in search of enlightenment.

We were staying at the same hotel where the week-long retreat was being held. The morning after we arrived, we were eager to start. We enjoyed breakfast and then walked over to the room to the workshop.

Once again, everyone was wearing white. The women wore long dresses with shawls, and the men wore long-sleeved white shirts and white pants. The newbies like myself and my friend were wearing brightly colored blouses and black pants. What showstoppers we were.

In the room, the men sat on one side and the women on the other. It was quiet as we were instructed to sit in meditation. Suddenly, everyone turned on their chairs to welcome her holiness Sai Maa Lakshmi Devi, who was standing in the doorway dressed in a magnificent white sari, with a smile that was larger than the moon.

She walked slowly to the front of the room, smiling and greeting those she knew. Her eyes were clear, luminous, and love seemed to flow out of her very being. She sat down on her special chair covered in a beautiful white, soft and pillowy fabric with white lights and flowers as the backdrop. She had a small footstool draped in the same fabric. She sat there for a while and just looked at all of us in the room. Her smile was filled with such love that just being in her presence prompted me to start crying again.

The most important thing I remember her saying was, "We are seeing a new awareness of who we are and why we have taken birth at this time in history." She also said we all would be assisted in this new shift so we could step into the Light Beings we truly are. We are all needed to shift the planet.

After the morning lesson, Sai Maa said she wished to meet with all the people here for the first time. Everyone who was new stood up, formed a line, and proceeded to get on their knees. Each person went up on their knees to be welcomed by her. I was so nervous, and as it got closer to my turn, I could hardly breathe. It was finally my turn, and I went up on my knees, kneeling before her. She looked into my eyes and said, "I've been waiting for you a long time, and

I'm so happy to see you." I finally believed I was in the right place. I had studied with others but never felt the connection as well as the recognition I felt with Sai Maa. I knew I was born to do something, but I didn't know what it was.

The afternoon session was amazing with chanting and dancing. The overflowing sense of joy on everyone's faces perpetuated more joy. At the end, they announced there was still room to sign up for a healing session that evening with Sai Maa. My friend and I decided it would be a golden opportunity and went up to put our names on the list. By the time we got there, we were told the list was full, but to put our room number down just in case there was a last-minute opening.

After dinner, I had just taken off my makeup, gotten into bed, and was almost asleep when the telephone rang. There was a vacancy and we could come to the room for our healing session. We quickly changed out of our pjs, combed our hair, and raced down excitedly to the assigned room. We waited in a room accompanying the healing room until it was our turn. I was called and led into the room. Placed on one of the massage tables and covered with a white sheet, someone even placed a sheet over my clothes. There I waited for Sai Maa with my eyes shut tight. My heart was just bursting with anticipation, and I was so grateful! I kept repeating, "Thank you, thank you, thank you." The feeling was overwhelming and wonderful, but it isn't easy to put into words. It was pure bliss. I felt Sai Maa's hands on my head. My breath stopped, and my heart was full once again. The energy she was sharing with me felt so wonderful and loving. It was beautiful. She said to the people who were assisting her, "Look at this woman's heart. It is overflowing with gratitude." She said to me, "I am placing a bright green pyramid inside your heart for you to remember gratitude is the fastest way to ascend."

I continued to lay in awe until someone assisted me up. I waited for my friend, who also had a wonderful experience, and we literally skipped back to our room, laughing like two four-year-old kids. We were both so giddy we had a difficult time falling asleep.

I learned so much that week about self-love and why we had taken birth. I felt a new sense of purpose. I felt a higher level of vibration when I returned home. I felt empowered, and it felt so good.

My friend and I attended two more week-long seminars with Sai Maa, and every time we came home, we were inspired to continue our journeys of enlightenment.

HOW MY ETHERIC AFFAIR CAME TO AN ABRUPT END

The second time we went to spend a week with Sai Maa, I got in trouble. First, I will explain what an etheric field is. The best definition I have found thus far is from Your Aura and Etheric Field by Jaya Sarada. He wrote:

"The etheric field is an electromagnetic grid that weaves around the physical field. There are thousands of tiny nerves that cross each other throughout the field. These nadis are threads of life force that underlie every part of the body. Where they cross, especially along the spine, they form the chakras, which are energy gateways which are described as wheels of light. The chakras are vital supports for the health of our multidimensional energy fields, affecting the way we feel physically, emotionally, mentally and spiritually."

At the beginning of my stepping into the spiritual gateway, I consulted with a spiritual therapist. She introduced me to the book, The Artist's Way. In one of my sessions with her, she said I would work with my 'higher self.' I learned in the etheric field my 'higher self' could ask another person's 'higher self' if he or she would receive the love I wanted to share with that person. The person would either give permission or not give permission. Subsequently, I explored by shutting my eyes, entering into a meditative state to access my 'higher self,' and addressing this question to three individuals, who all gave their permission to receive my gift of love. Sending love to another in this way was such a beautiful experience, as I could feel the flow going from my heart to their hearts. It warm and glorious.

Within my further exploration, I asked my supervisor at the time, if her higher self would like the gift of love. There was an immediate reaction where she clearly said, "No, I do not want any love. I can do it myself." That was different, and it was powerful as I felt the "no" clearly in my body. These explorations taught me one could send love and healing to another through the person's etheric body if given permission.

Now back to the affair. I was in a week-long seminar with my guru at the time, Sai Maa. As I said before, she comes from pure love and compassion, assisting individuals with enlightening toward Truth. As I sat in my chair listening to Sai Maa, I noticed an attractive man sitting across the aisle. He had gray hair, a nice body, and seemed sexy. One night, as I lay in my bed, I decided to ask him if he wanted to have an etheric affair, as I thought it wouldn't hurt anyone, and it would be fun. So, I did. I proceeded to ask his higher self if he was interested. I got the answer. His higher self said, "Yes." Hot dog, my first etheric affair. Off I went to sleep. This went on for few nights until one night, when I again asked his higher self, and he said, "No." Whoops!

The following day, I was seated, waiting for Sai Maa to arrive for the day. I closed my eyes when I felt her presence in front of me. She said to me, "Stop doing that right now." I immediately knew what she was referring to. I opened my eyes, but she was not there. She entered the room fifteen minutes later. Her spirit had spoken to me. My etheric affair was terminated, and I was in serious trouble. Seated in the second row, I never thought she would know what I was doing, but I was wrong. But I have to tell you while it happened, it was fun.

I SENT A PRAYER REQUEST TO SAI MAA IN THE ETHER

In 2020, I went to India just as the pandemic started in China. India is a very special place, the people are kind and welcoming. The food was delicious and the experiences we had on this trip were magical and fun. The adventure started in New Delhi and we traveled to many places including the Taj Mahal, which was incredible. But as much as I loved seeing where we went, I couldn't wait until we arrived in Lucknow where the Bengal Tigers live. Before I left, I sent a silent prayer to Sai Maa, asking her to please keep me safe.

I'M GOING TO SEE A TIGER TODAY... HOORAH, HOORAH

We arrived in Lucknow in the late afternoon and immediately boarded a jeep to see if we would encounter any tigers. This was tiger country, and I was excited. It was nearing dusk when we all heard a sharp cry. Our guide said it was from a deer, indicating a predator was nearby. The predator was a leopard, and it was dragging a deer into the brush. A few members on the trip said they saw the incident, but thankfully, I didn't. Unfortunately, we did not see any tigers. Other groups came back to the lodge thrilled, boasting how many tigers they had seen during the afternoon.

We watched a movie in the evening about the tigers that live in the area and what they do, their names, and so forth, but I was still disappointed. Then, our guide said if we wanted to go back early in the morning we might have another chance to spot a tiger. I absolutely hate getting up early, and 5:00 a.m. is sacrilegious. So, what did I do? I set my alarm. I just had to see a tiger in the wild.

Once again, the alarm went off at 5:00 a.m. I stumbled out of bed, put on every stitch of warm clothing I brought with me, grabbed a cup of coffee, and got into the jeep. Outside it was pitch black and quite cold. The guide gave us blankets, and off we went. While snuggled under the blanket as we drove past the monkeys and birds, I started to quietly sing a song I made up for this very moment. The song went, "We are going to see a tiger today hurrah, hurrah." Of course, I did not share the song with the rest of the group but continued singing it to myself until...

Lynn, I said to myself, What happens if you don't see a tiger today? How disappointed will you be?

It was then that I remembered how the universe tests us. Patterns will always show up until you see them and break the pattern. This pattern was "don't be attached to the outcome." It was a lesson I had repeated a lot, and here it was once again.

Thank goodness I became aware of what I was doing in the nick of time. I reprogramed myself and said, "If you see a tiger, that will be wonderful, and if not, you can enjoy riding in a jeep seeing other animals in this beautiful forest." I stopped singing my song and started observing just how beautiful the forest was. The sun peeked out, and the day warmed up. All was good in the world.

How often had I taught this in my classes, 'Don't be attached to the outcome'? You can ask for what you desire, but then just let it go.

It wasn't much later when our guide said he was tracking a tiger. I was so excited at the news I held my breath. Sure enough, just a few minutes after he made the remark, a majestic, beautiful female tiger emerged from the forest behind the jeep. My heart almost jumped out of my chest, tears flowed from my eyes, and I offered a prayer of gratitude. I was so excited; there she was in full view following our jeep.

She just stood there watching us as we all kept taking pictures of her. She was magnificent. The tears continued flowing, and I know she looked directly at me before she walked away into the forest.

We saw many people in cars looking at something in the forest on our way back to the camp, so we pulled our jeep over to the side. Lo and behold, a mother tiger and her two cubs were walking toward our jeep. What a sight! I was overjoyed. It was more than I could ever have imagined.

Gratitude flowed through my heart.

NEXT STOP: VARANASI

I couldn't wait to get to Varanasi, as it is considered one of the oldest continually inhabited cities globally on the banks of the River Ganges. Moreover, it is one of the most sacred sites in India because it is believed to have been the home of Lord Shiva. According to Hindu beliefs, Shiva is the Supreme Lord who creates, protects, and transforms the universe.

It is not a city that is clean or polished, but it is an incredible place. There are thousands of individuals near the river. You see people with backpacks, holy men chanting and meditating, tourists from all different countries, monkeys jumping across the rooftops, and straying dogs. For me, this city was magical.

The Hindus believe in reincarnation, and if a person dies and is cremated at the River Ganges, he or she will be free from the cycle of rebirth. Therefore, many individuals travel great distances to cremate their beloved family member in the river.

Our group arrived just before the sun was setting where we immediately boarded a boat which took us to the cremation ghats. We witnessed how they prepared the body before cremation. Unique wood was used, so there were no unpleasant smells. The rituals practiced here for the dead have been going for centuries. Observing the living traditions of one of the world's oldest and most populated religions was an incredible experience. Finally, we watched as the body was cremated, and we lit small candles and sent them out of the boat with our prayers.

We went further up the Ganges to witness the daily sunset rituals. It is here where light is offered up to the Hindus deities. Hundreds of people sit and stand at this ritual. The holy men chant and light their lamps with fire that can be seen for miles.

After dinner, our guide invited us for sunrise over the Ganges. Everyone who has ever gone says the sunrise over the Ganges is not to be missed as it is a magical experience. The only problem for me was once again I had to get up at the ungodly hour of 5:00 a.m. But when would I ever be back in India? So, I signed up for a 4:45 a.m. wakeup call.

The alarm went off at 4:45 a.m. Chickens may like to rise at this hour, but I don't. So, out of bed, I dressed quickly and went down to board the bus with a few more of my fellow travelers as we headed there once again for a new adventure.

It was a cool morning, and there were only a few people around. We walked from our bus along the shop-lined streets of Varanasi as people were starting their day. The steps going down to the river are ancient and large, and for a short-legged woman like me, they are challenging, as my flexibility has lessened over the years. One of the men on the trip was kind enough to escort me down the large steps when another man appeared. He was young, maybe just twenty years old, and he insisted on taking my arm while I climbed down to the river. I told him I didn't have any money, but he said he was doing dharma. Which means 'doing good' in assisting me, who he referred to as an older lady. Normally, I might have protested, but I was still half-asleep.

I keep forgetting I am considered an old lady. In my mind, I am forever young. It's just the body that refuses to cooperate. The gray hairs are also present.

We walked slowly arm-in-arm down the stairs to the river. The boat we had taken the night before was waiting for our group. The young man said he would see me at my next stop. Our group boarded the boat just as the sun began to rise. One could see just a tiny speck of the sun peeking out over the river on the horizon. It rose out of and above the river. As the seconds passed, the sun appeared in increments until there was this liquid golden ball of sunlight glittering the waters off the Ganges. It was worth getting up so early for this beautiful sight.

As we continued the trip down the river, we could see many people performing a ceremony as they splashed in the river. Our guide said this is a ritual for the cleansing of their sins. They dip three times in the Ganges to cleanse. The women dipped fully dressed in bright saris and took little silver jugs to collect the Ganga water for later. It was a magical experience.

We stopped to observe the city, and the young man appeared once again to assist me in getting off the boat and walking back up the stairs. He told me about his family. His mother passed away when he was a young child, and his father took care of him and his younger sister. He could speak seven languages, and his job was to earn money for his family by selling his stickers and postcards. It was a story one might hear all over India. Poverty was rampant, and people were struggling.

As we walked back up the stairs to my bus, he showed me what he was selling. Again, I said I didn't have any money. He said: "This is a present for you," as he handed me his gifts.

He then asked me if I liked India. I started to tell him I had studied with a guru for about five years and how she was the mother of love, and her name was Sai Maa Lakshmi Devi. He stopped abruptly and pulled out a picture from his wallet. It was Sai Maa. He studied with her as well, as she was his guru.

Out of millions of people living in Varanasi, Sai Maa had shown up to take care of me through this young man. I remembered my silent prayer.

Before I embraced going on this new adventure, I had sent out a prayer to my guru, Sai Maa Lakshmi Devi, asking her to please watch over me while I was visiting India. For good measures, I also put in the same request to Sai Baba.

My silent prayer was heard, and I was in bliss. I knew I was being heard every single time experiences like this happened to me—what an incredible feeling of gratitude.

At the bus, we said goodbye, and I gave him all the money I had taken with me for the day. Obviously, Sai Maa wanted me to take good care of this young man.

ANOTHER LESSON FROM AARON

In 1999, my daughter was planning to get married, and I decided it was an excellent time to get plastic surgery on my eyes. They were getting a little droopy, and I wanted to look my best at the wedding. I was all prepared, I made a hypnotherapy tape for myself not only for relaxation purposes but for healing. I told myself, I was going to go back to work in eight days. I came home from the surgery and was taking great care of myself. I put ice compacts on my eyes, took my medicine, and used all my healing practices to encourage a very speedy recovery. I looked better every day, and this gave me more incentive to continue with my practices. But I was surprised on Saturday when I looked into the mirror and saw what appeared to be two very red eyes staring back at me. The first word out of my mouth was a swear word.

On Sunday, I got up and I looked no better; I swore again, and I phoned the surgeon to ask for some medication as I was sure I had a bacterial infection in my eyes. He prescribed some eye drops and said he would see me on Monday morning. I was right on time for my appointment. My looks that morning would have scared anyone. There I sat with two bright red eyes and no makeup. I could have been in a horror film.

I think I scared the doctor. He prescribed more drops, plus an antibiotic cream. He also recommended I call my eye doctor if my eyes didn't get any better. I left the office feeling down, depressed, and most of all, scared. I went to get my prescriptions filled and waited patiently for them to take effect and perform a miracle on my eyes. Nothing happened. Now, I was scared I was going blind, and my face was ruined, and I would be disfigured for my daughter's wedding. (Thank God I never became a doctor because medical school would have killed me. I would have thought that a splinter not removed would have been gangrene and sure death.)

I had taken care of myself; I used Reiki as well as my added shamanic healing but to no avail. I decided I needed to write to Aaron, my guide, to see what he had to say. This is what Aaron wrote, "You are being asked to practice what you preach and trust you are living in a very responsive universe that hears your every prayer. This is a test in letting go, and you will be LED just like you tell the others. Lynn, you do not have control, and patience is still a number one issue for you. Let go. You will be happy with the results of your eyes. You will be pleased you had the surgery. Allow yourself time to heal. Quiet your mind and body and let the healing process go on as you have nothing to fear. You see, all your wishes come to fruition, don't you?" "Yes," I replied, so why question it now? The reason you question is you don't truly trust yet. Just surrender and trust. Believe me, you are in good hands. God hears your prayers just like everyone else's. Relax, create, be still, and wait. You will see a transpire overnight. Trust, and it will be. That's all I have to say."

And he was right on.

LEARNING ABOUT DEATH

> ***"What the caterpillar calls the end of the world the master calls a butterfly"***
>
> ~ **Richard Bach**

I have come to realize through my experiences a death is merely another transition. Our bodies may die, but our soul continues to live on. Energy never dies.

PREMONITIONS: FIRST STEP

Death scared me when I was young, as I had premonitions about it. The unknown is very frightening at any age, and then you receive valuable information that death is not what you thought at all.

As I was writing this, I asked Aaron to let me know how I felt at twelve years old when I found out my father had died.

He said, "You could not fathom the thought of death. It was so abstract, and you had no model of grief, so when your father's death happened, you buried the grief, and it showed up in different ways."

While walking home from school one day when I was young, a scary thought entered my mind, and it really frightened me. I have no recollection of how a thought about death should enter my mind, but it did. The thought was when you die, you die forever and ever and ever and ever and ever. I still can remember and viscerally feel the moment it happened. I didn't know how to stop saying forever, and ever and it really scared me. However, once I started singing a song, the thought disappeared, and life went back to normal, or so I thought.

A weird thing happened to me one afternoon as I was looking out of the living room window. I experienced another very disturbing thought. The thought was that my father was going to die soon. As a twelve-year-old, I had never experienced such a scary thought and again buried it. What I experienced on that day was, in fact, a premonition. The definition of a premonition is a strong feeling that something is going to happen.

After the initial premonition, I continued to have premonitions on and off throughout my life. I'd be doing something random, and, suddenly, a thought would enter my mind, and I knew something bad was going to happen. I began to trust those thoughts, and something always did happen. Once, a car was sliding into my lane on a freeway with two of my little children sitting in the backseat. Another time on a family vacation, we took a ferry to Victoria, Canada, from Seattle, Washington, when I had a very strong premonition. This thought really scared me as I do not swim well, and we were on a ferry boat. My brother and sister-in-law and my husband were on this trip with our two small children. I know they thought I was loony, but I told them the ferry would be in trouble soon. I asked my brother to take my son and my husband to take our daughter if something happened. Not a minute later, the ferry hit very rough waters and everyone on this ferry had difficulty staying seated. The ferry was rocking back and forth. I thought for sure we were going to overturn. We finally landed in Victoria, and all went well. That is until we returned to our car in Seattle going home. Suddenly, a rock hit the front window and caused it to break and then the car's lights came on indicating there was an engine problem. Instead of driving home, we ended up spending the night in a motel. The next day the engine light did not go on, and we drove home. Premonition over. Phew!

I have continued to have premonitions throughout the years, and I always pay attention because something always happened. One Saturday evening, when my husband and I were invited to a dinner honoring the Council General of Spain, I had another very powerful premonition. It was a strong sense something was going to happen, and from previous experiences, I knew it was likely to be bad, so I wasn't thrilled about going to this fundraiser. But my friends were running the fundraiser, and I couldn't disappoint them. I quickly got dressed, and off we went.

As I recall, dinner was delicious, and after dinner, there was a presentation and a show. Later, there was a raffle for two tickets and hotel accommodations for a one-week trip to Spain. You could feel the excitement before the name was pulled out of the bowl. The emcee mixed up all of the names and pulled one out. The winner of the trip to Spain with airfare included is..., and I knew deep inside we had won. I held my breath, and lo and behold, we won the trip. It was an incredible ending of my negative premonitions. Someone upstairs wanted me to understand premonitions can be viewed as a warning system for good and not-so-good experiences. I always listen.

Looking back at these experiences, I realize I always listened to these feelings and messages. I know now it was my inner voice talking to me. Then, I didn't have a clue, but I listened anyway. These experiences were building my listening skills to listen and trust my inner dialogue. And I do.

MY FIRST "WOO WOO" DEATH STORY

The time finally came when I discovered death wasn't what I thought it was. Instead, it was something far greater than I could ever imagine.

In the winter of life, my mother lived alone in Chicago. She continued to work with my brother in the men's wholesale business until she was seventy years old. Winter in Chicago is not fun. It is cold, snowy, and blistery. That's why my mom would hop on a plane and visit us in Northern California, where she spent the winters, and we were thrilled to have her. Not only did she make a great salad for dinner every night, but she would also customize a special one for my daughter, who only liked carrots and lettuce in her salad.

(Now, my daughter is a mother, and she has been blessed with a daughter who also follows her tradition of not liking many things. I wonder if that would be considered karma?)

As my mother got older, she would spend more time in California. The two dogs and the cat kept her company during the day, and everyone was home for dinner.

One summer, Mom returned to her home in Chicago, became very sick, and was diagnosed with emphysema. My brother and his family took care of her, but they both worked full time. My brother and I decided it would be a better option if she came to live with my family and me. We had a big room downstairs, and we moved the furniture out to make this room her bedroom.

The first weekend my mom arrived, the bathroom downstairs overflowed, and all we could do was turn off the water. We called Roto Rooter, and the plumber said he could fix it but would have to tear up the backyard to get to the outside pipes on the street. There appeared to be a crack between the house and the street. This diagnosis was not very appealing, so we called a different plumber who said he could fix our issue by going into the basement and out the cement wall to the main pipe. We thought this was a better option, so they started work on Monday. They fixed the problem with the toilet so my mother could use the bathroom. However, in order to do so, a very large garbage can with a bag in it had to be placed beneath the basement toilet. Once she went to the bathroom, we would then remove the bag, toss it into the trash, and replace the can with a new bag. This process was our only option as my mother could not walk up the stairs.

On Monday morning, they started drilling, and I will never forget it. I stayed home from work to take care of my mom, and all I heard was what sounded like a submachine gun repeatedly being fired through the cement wall. At the same time, my mother complained that her hearing aids were not working and needed to have them fixed. I left the house with her hearing aids in hand, no makeup on, uncombed hair, and went to the hearing aid store. I was sitting in the waiting room, looking like a crazy woman talking to myself and mumbling about everything that was happening. Regardless of how I looked or what I was saying, the store associates took pity on me and gave me batteries. Once again, I was home, my mother could hear, and the machine-gun-going-through-cement sound was loud and even more annoying. The job took four days, and by that time, I couldn't wait to get back to work. Also, I am sure my mother was not happy that her hearing aids worked during all the commotion.

AU PAIR AND SOMEONE ELSE?

Eventually, I hired someone to take care of my mom while I was at work. I also had an au pair living in the house who made sure my mom was okay. One evening, one of my friends told me about a psychic she had spoken to and wanted to know if I might be interested in speaking with her as well. I thought about it, and I called her because I wanted to know how long my mother had left before she would pass away. The psychic told me many stories about how we had been together in other lives, and in this lifetime, she was my mother, and I had been her mother in other lives. She said to me that I had to let her go in order for my mother to pass away. I really didn't understand what that meant at the time. The psychic also told me the young girl was coming to get my mom—she was part of her family but had died young—and that my mother would pass away when I let her go. This made no sense to me, but I didn't ask her what I had to do to let her go. I thought the conversation was really interesting, and I went downstairs to tell my mom what the psychic said. I told her we had been together in other lives, and I told her about the young girl coming to get her when it was time to go to heaven. She didn't know any young girls who had died. She wanted to call the psychic back and ask her questions, but we never did.

On the weekends, part of my job was taking care of my mother from seven o'clock in the morning until two o'clock in the afternoon. As the months wore on, I grew tired and stressed out. It was hard for me to do both jobs, one as a social worker and the other as a caregiver. So, I finally said I was hiring a woman to start coming in on the weekends to help me.

Soon after deciding to hire someone to assist me, I was in for a big surprise. I arrived home from work, gave my mom a kiss even though she was sort of in and out of consciousness by this time, and I started making dinner. My husband wasn't home for dinner that evening. I made Chinese chicken salad for the three of us—my mother's caregiver, the au pair, and myself. We were sitting and eating dinner when we all heard what appeared to be a young girl talking to my mom in her room. We stopped eating and looked at each other. Neither a television nor a radio was on. The three of us literally sat frozen at the table, all humming the song from Rod Sterling's television show The Twilight Zone. We were afraid to walk into her room but finally, we did. Thank goodness no little girl was present, or I would have fainted.

In a very clear voice, my mother told me she was going to die that evening. I was flabbergasted, but all I said was, "Go in peace, mom, I love you." I have absolutely no idea where the phrase came from. I probably should have spent a lot more time telling her she was such a wonderful and loving mom as well as a fantastic grandmother. But I simply said to go in peace. At least I told her that I loved her. By asking for help, I had let go; that was what she had been waiting for.

I was afraid to sit downstairs with her. I don't know why but I just was. So, I asked the caregiver to let me know when she was in the final stages of dying so I could be with her.

At 3:30 a.m. the next morning, the caregiver came to wake me up and let me know my mother had passed away. I was really disappointed in myself that I was too afraid to sit with her as death came. But at least I knew she was with the young girl.

I didn't hear from my mother for a very long time and then she surprised me.

A BUSHEL AND A PECK AND A HUG AROUND THE NECK...

A friend of mine recently lost her husband. She was at his bedside as he began his transition. In a brief conversation we had before he passed away, I suggested she ask him to let her know he was okay after he passed.

It has been my experience that newly deceased individuals will often contact their loved ones and let them know they are all right. It doesn't always happen, but when it does, it gives a person peace of mind. One friend saw her husband sitting on the sofa where he always sat one evening when she returned home, and he smiled at her. She was too scared at the moment and went to her room. But she knew she saw him and he looked well. Another friend saw her mother in a particular bird that always came to visit after she had died. She knew it was her mom.

People share their stories with me because they think I will understand and not look at them as if they are crazy. I have friends who were present when their dear rabbi was in the process of passing away. His adored wife died some years earlier, and they always said they were soul mates. He slowly closed his eyes while he held my friend's hand as he passed away. She said at the moment he died, there was a loud whoosh sound and a white light full of sparkles arching out of his chest up and out of the hospital room.

She said, and I quote, "If my husband wasn't with me watching this, I would have thought I made it up." But it's true, we saw it, and we know he is happy in heaven with his wife. The only person she could tell this to was me. I am what she calls her woo woo spiritual advisor, and she knew I would believe her.

In my own life, I have been blessed to hear from my father and from my aunt, who each told me they were all right, but I had not heard from my mother until Saturday night, June 26, 2010. I remember it clearly as my husband

and I were celebrating our forty-fifth wedding anniversary. Earlier in the day, I had been fondly remembering our wedding day when we were so young. I revisited the night forty-five years earlier when we took our vows in front of so many family members and friends. I thought about the many family members who had been at the wedding and were no longer living.

Now, forty-five years later, we were going out for dinner with friends to celebrate our anniversary. As I pulled out of the garage, I turned on the radio. To our delight and surprise, our wedding song was playing. As it played, it would stop, then start again, and sound scratchy. The entirety of the song did not play continuously or steadily. My husband and I thought the same thing, What are the chances of our wedding song playing at that exact moment, and who sent it to us? Like many other couples at that time, our wedding song was the song "More." What are the odds of this happening? Not only was this a gift, but a really big synchronicity. We were both enthralled by the experience.

Having already forgotten about the synchronicity, another one was about to occur on the following Tuesday morning, after my Jazzercise class. As I was walking my dog in the park, I was trying to figure out how old my mother was when I got married. Unfortunately, I am not a math genius, and thus it was taking me a long time to compute the numbers. That was the last thought I had when I got into the car to go home.

As I turned on the radio, the song "A Bushel and a Peck" was playing. I never heard this song played before. Apparently, this song was a very popular one in 1950, and this was the phrase my mother would use to tell her children and her grandchildren she loved them. At the end of every conversation, she would sign off by saying, "I love you, a bushel and a peck, and a hug around the neck." It was her trademark. It was my mom. She had finally shown up and had learned how to communicate by radio. Not only was I excited but I was so proud of her accomplishment. She sent us the song for our anniversary.

MY DAD COMES TO MY RESCUE

I was brought up in a small but very loving family. My Aunt Sylvia and Uncle Morrie were a big part of my life, especially after my father had passed away. My uncle would assist me with my math problems, and he didn't tear his hair out while doing so. (As you know from another story, math has never been my strength.) They both taught my brother and me how to ski, which was very challenging, but they stuck it out and were wonderful to us. I have many delightful memories of my times with them, even when they made us wear boots when it rained.

My Uncle Morrie died in July 1999, and my Uncle Al soon followed him. Again, I felt so bad I was not with them in the final moments of their lives. My aunt then died a few years later. And again, I could not be present and felt a deep sense of remorse.

My worry about them and what happened to them weighed heavily on me until one night when my Aunt Mildred, my mother's oldest sister, came to me in a dream. There was a knock on my bedroom door in the dream, and when I opened it, there she stood with a huge bouquet of flowers in her arms. She was wearing a tailored suit, small pumps, and her hair was just like she used to wear it. In the dream, I knew she was not living, and I started to cry. She handed me the flowers and said not to worry about the family as they were all okay. I still remember the dream clearly. I woke up feeling like a load had been taken off my heart.

Soon after my aunt's death, my brother and I met in Florida to help liquidate my Aunt Sylvia and Uncle Morrie's condo and go through all the pictures, artwork, and their many albums.

Before I boarded my plane in San Francisco to head to Florida, I set an intention. At times, my brother can be very volatile, and admittedly, I often egg him on. I did not want this to happen, so I set my intention that I would not lose my balance; I would keep my energy high and not let anything bother me. There are a few individuals in the world who know how to push every button I have, and one of them happens to be my brother. I was determined not to cave in and not to react to anything that came up.

My brother met me at the airport, and the very next morning, we left for the condo. Of course, neither of us had the key, but I was keeping my cool. Soon, someone emerged from the building and let us in. I was prepared for the condo to have a decaying smell, but the condo smelled just like my aunt and uncle. It was a very familiar smell and somewhat comforting.

On the first day there, my brother and I started looking through piles and piles of photographs. There was a picture of me standing next to my mechanical dog when I was eight years old, which I found hysterical. Who but my dear aunt and uncle would have a picture of my mechanical dog? I started to laugh looking at that photo—there I stood, as proud as proud could be, next to my mechanical dog that I held by the leash. My dog walked, nodded his head, and barked. As the afternoon went on, we continued to find many treasures and boxed some of them up.

The next morning, my brother woke up in a grumpy mood. I was very conscious not to do or say anything that might push him. We went back to our aunt and uncle's condo and began sorting what we wanted to take. I wanted everything, and he didn't want very much. He was getting restless and walked into the Florida room with louvered windows that faced the seventeenth hole on the golf course. As soon as he walked into the room, he lifted the louvers and began shouting at an elderly man playing golf. With much anger in his voice, he yelled, "Why are you in such a hurry?! You are only going to die anyway!"

I was in the living room packing when I heard him yelling. I immediately started praying loudly to myself. In my head, I was praying for my family members, my guides, my angels, and my teachers to come down immediately to help me out.

My brother came back into the living room and went to the bathroom. I prayed harder for assistance, and when he came out, I gently said, "It is not good for you to get so emotional. You could have a heart attack or stroke." He responded, "I know, but I have a hard time saying goodbye." I knew exactly what he was referring to because he was nine years old when our father died, and he never processed Dad's death. He buried all his feelings, and this turned into anger. Now, in this condo, he had become his nine-year-old self again and didn't have the tools to handle a loved one passing. He was in emotional pain as he had never dealt with our father's death. I said to him, "Let's go do something that would be fun for you. We could go to the flea market in town." He said, "No, let's pack this stuff up and take it to the post office." As we finished packing, I asked my brother if he ever thought about our father. He said, "Yes, whenever I smell cigar smoke." I responded that I did too; every time I smell cigars, I know Dad is with me.

We went down the elevator with the boxes and he got the car while I waited by the door. When returned, there was a very potent smell of cigar smoke in the air. I asked whether he could smell it. He said he could, and I said, "Dad's here." My brother could hardly believe his nose and the strong smell of cigar. He looked all over the entire condominium and in the ashtrays, and no one was around. I told him, "Dad is here and he's telling you to lighten up."

Off we went to Saratoga to see our cousins. It was a three-hour drive, and because I had set my intention to be loving and light, I talked the entire way there. In one of my monologues, I said I wondered if they had eagles in Florida. I've always wanted to see an eagle. Thank goodness I was even getting tired of my monologues. When my cousin opened the door and saw the expression on my face, she offered me a drink. I immediately said, "Yes." That vodka tonic was a blessing, and I was officially off duty keeping the energy up.

As we were having breakfast on our cousins' lanai the next morning, an eagle flew over the pond in the marsh behind their house. My mouth was open as the eagle came back, swooped down with talons projected into the pond, and swooped up again. I was crying, and my brother knew I called in the eagle.

It was my turn to drive the three hours back to Pompano Beach to lock up my aunt and uncle's house. Driving back, I commented with a huge smile, "Well, what do you think? First, I brought in Dad, and next, we saw an eagle." He was quiet for a moment and then said, "Are you a witch?" And we both laughed.

Upon entering their condo for the last time, I immediately noticed a distinct smell similar to rotten eggs. Their smell wasn't present anymore as their spirits had left. This experience comforted me. I knew they had been there with us.

Getting on the plane to go back to California, I took a long inward breath, and sighed. I was proud of myself for not reflecting anger back to my brother. I kept my intention. I stayed balanced without any attachment to the outcome—what a gift.

DREAMS CAN BE VERY CONSOLING

After returning home to the Bay Area, I felt sad we had no memorial or celebration of their lives. My other uncle also had died, and I didn't know about it for a few days.

All of them had signed up for the Neptune society, and their ashes were scattered at sea. Unfortunately, none of our family was there to send them on their new journey. They all played such an important role in my brother's life and in my life. My Aunt Sylvia always took care of us and made us wear our boots to school even if we hated them, and Uncle Al, who never passed up a time to pinch our cheeks.

Shortly thereafter, I had a consoling dream. I was sound asleep, and I heard a knock on my bedroom door. The door opened, and there stood my Aunt Mildred who had died a long time ago. I started to cry as I knew she was dead. But there she stood, just like I remembered her in her forties. She had on her pillbox hat, her perfectly fitted suit, and her signature pumps.

In her arms, she carried the most magnificent bouquet of flowers and she handed them to me. She told me everyone was doing well and not to worry about them. I woke up that morning with a feeling of great relief. Our dreams carry significant messages for us, and we just need to pay attention. Of course, we often don't understand them, but they are powerful when we do.

TWO VERY SIGNIFICANT DEATHS

Michael, my husband of fifty-two years, died in February 2017, and my daughter-in-law passed away three months later in May. Michael had been ill for a long time and was in a lot of pain. He had a myriad of diseases, including diabetes, heart fibrillation, leukemia, and gout. He had been in and out of hospitals and convalescent homes for a while. I knew it was time to bring him home to his own house surrounded by the people he loved. My family could give him more loving care. I set up a room for him and ordered a hospital bed, bed table, walker, and everything else we needed. I called Hospice, and I hired a family care worker to assist me.

Michael was on a multitude of heavy drugs, but nothing seemed to alleviate his pain. The pain continued to get worse.

I didn't know how to help him, and that saddened my heart. The night before he passed away, I decided to send a prayer to my mother. I said, "Mom, you loved Michael, and he loved you; please come down and get him. He is in so much pain." Although I wasn't fond of his parents, and that is another story, I felt I needed to ask them to come down also.

The following day, I went downstairs, and his caretaker said to me, "Did you come down last night to talk to Michael?" I said I hadn't. She said she had woken up and saw what she thought was me having a private moment with Michael. She didn't want to disturb me but called my name. She said I didn't answer her. I said I wasn't there. She then asked me if I had a white nightgown with rosebuds on it. I didn't wear nightgowns, and I didn't own one with rosebuds on it. I asked her if the nightgown was long or short and if it had sleeves or didn't have sleeves. I asked these questions because my mother wore only short nightgowns with no sleeves and my mother-in-law only wore long nightgowns with long sleeves (even in the summer). She said the nightgown was long with long sleeves, and I knew then that my mother-in-law had come to help her son transition.

That same morning, Michael took his last breath and I was there to witness his passing. I held his hand and kissed him, but I don't believe he was in his body. I believe he left with his mother the night before. He looked so peaceful and handsome, and he was no longer in excruciating pain. It was truly a blessing.

My daughter-in-law, Maria, was a beautiful, bright, and loving woman who was diagnosed with triple-negative breast cancer. This was heartbreaking for all of us. Maria and my son had been married for thirteen years when she passed away. Their son, Deven, was thirteen years old.

Maria had been raised Catholic but was non-practicing. When she became really ill, she once again turned back to her religion. I assisted her with guided meditations asking both Jesus and Mother Mary to help with her healings. She was comforted by the meditations, but at the end of her life, her biggest concern was that she didn't see God, and this made her sad. No matter what her family or I said to her, she was not happy. I told her God was an energy of pure love and that although she couldn't see God, she could feel that loving energy. She just didn't believe me.

After Michael and Maria passed away, a dear friend of mine gifted me a session with an individual who communicated with deceased beings. I sent her a picture of Michael and Maria. She knew absolutely nothing about either of them.

On the day of my appointment, I called her. I do not believe all psychics are legitimate; they have to prove to me they are actually communicating with my loved ones.

This is what the psychic said immediately: Maria was present, and Michael was standing next to her. Maria was quite concerned that her son was not getting the proper care because he was playing video games and not doing his homework. Then she added that Maria is so excited she wants me to tell Ya Ya (their name for me) there is a God, there really is a God; it doesn't look anything like I thought it would, but there is a God. You were right. And Michael piped in, saying, "All your woo woo stuff (that's what he called my spirituality work) that you've been doing for years is right. Keep on doing it."

I knew both Michael and Maria sent their messages as the psychic would have never known about Maria's search for God or that Michael called what I was doing, woo woo stuff. My heart was full of gratitude, knowing I had the opportunity to understand that these two beautiful individuals I loved very much had transitioned and were still around me.

THE HARD LESSON OF DISCERNMENT: WHAT I LEARNED ABOUT ME

Everything was going along smoothly. I was led to the right teachers, the right books, and the most extraordinary experiences. Then a big lesson happened—a lesson of discernment. Of course, I had no idea it was a lesson until it was over, and I could see what transpired. I really don't think I had learned about being discerning. I must have missed that lesson. But in retrospect, I certainly knew right from wrong. Apparently, I was so intent about connecting with some of my spiritual teachers that I didn't see how I was being used—lack of discernment.

What is discernment? According to Merriam-Webster, the definition is: "The ability to see and understand people, things, or situations clearly and intelligently as in reading character or motives." You would think I had a lot of discernment as a social worker, but I am not sure it was there either.

As I was writing this story, I checked in with Aaron, my guide, to see what he had to add to this lesson. Here is what he said: "It is all going as planned. You have acquired a deeper understanding of wounds that operate at an unconscious level. Your experience and lessons with discernment were all based upon the belief that you were not enough. So, what you did was extend your heart, home, and kindness more than once, thinking these individuals would be your friends. Never once did you think these individuals were just takers and using you. When your unconscious mind puts out a vibration such as I will assist you, and you don't know to look back to see what is really happening, the lesson will keep repeating until you see what is showing up in your life that you no longer want. When you get the message and the lesson, you will no longer feel powerless and vulnerable to those individuals who will take advantage of your kindness. Then you can step out of not being enough and a place of vulnerability, and step into a new place with the knowledge that you are so much more than enough. With that lesson comes discernment. You step into the uniqueness of who you are."

In 1999, I traveled to Egypt with twenty-four healers and my husband. Out of the twenty-four, there were shamans, channelers, an Egyptian author, and me—a want-to-be. I was so excited to go to this amazing country that had so many antiquities. Our hotel was near the Sphinx and the Pyramids. Viewing it the very first time was magical. My heart was racing, and tears flowed down my face as I gazed upon this magnificent monument. Standing in the Sahara Desert with the sun on my face and the winds blowing a magical pattern of sand all around me was very comforting. It felt familiar, and I loved the feelings I was experiencing. I had a very strong feeling I had been there before.

This story isn't about my Egyptian experience; it is my story of learning discernment. I had been on a course of following all my leads and enjoying every single one of them. I felt safe as well as supported. My guides decided it was now time to learn discernment and didn't bother to give me any 'heads up.' I also had a major lesson in self-esteem. These were difficult lessons.

I looked up to this group of women and two men. I felt they had more power and knowledge than I. I was playing small and didn't realize I was setting myself up for being left out.

Being left out is another significant issue for me. I hate being left out, and it stems from nursery school when the other children at my pre-school wouldn't play with me, and I didn't know how to handle the situation. So, here I was in this group playing small and feeling very sorry for myself. Even one of my closest friends went to play with the group's prominent leaders, leaving me out. I was sad and licking my wounds. One of the women on the trip asked if I would like to talk with her. She was kind and sensed I was having some difficulty. I took the opportunity to share all of my woes with her and told her my story. She said I needed to learn discernment. I wasn't sure what I was supposed to discern. I wasn't even sure I knew what discernment was. I have since learned it is the ability to judge people and things well. My mistake was thinking every one of these powerful healers were kind and supportive and knew more than I did. Oh boy, was I learning the lesson of discernment.

I AM A WORKER BEE

After I returned home from Egypt, I received a group text from one of the women on the trip. She wrote she would be in San Francisco for a class and inquired if anybody could house her for the weekend. Four individuals from that trip lived near or in San Francisco. Yet, no one responded except me.

Intuitively, I felt her dislike of me. I probably reminded her of someone in her life, but that didn't stop me from hosting her as no one else volunteered. I was still into the "take advantage of me" phase.

She took me up on my offer and came late in the evening. She spent the next day in a class on Shamanic Studies with one of the leaders from our Egypt trip. She came back for dinner, and everything was fine. After dinner, we went outside in my backyard, as it was a warm and lovely evening in Northern California. We sat together looking at the stars and drinking wine. That's when she said, and I quote: "There are Queen bees, and then there are worker bees." She continued, "I am a Queen bee, and you are a worker bee." I have no idea what I said in response, but it hurt my feelings. What the hell! I sat there in my backyard with my mouth open and listened to her proclaim her majesty. The next day, she returned to class, and after dinner that evening, she asked if I would drive her to Oakland the next day. I said, "No." She could take BART to Oakland, and that is what she did. On the way to the station, she said I reminded her of her mother, and my retort was, "I would never have raised a child like you." I got my big-girl pants on and stood up for myself. She was unkind, and I needed to be more discerning in my life. I knew she did not like me from the time we first met.

Years later, as I was drying my hair (inviting moments of inspiration), I remembered the "Queen bee" story and how it hurt my feelings. I realized that good old queen bees have sex once and then spend the rest of their time fertilizing the eggs until the sperm runs out. Then, when they no longer have fertilization ability, they just sit on their happy tushes all day long, waiting to be fed by the worker bees.

Now, according to my research, worker bees have several roles they play within the hive. They nurse and care for the young bees as well as the queen. They act as housekeepers whose job is to clean and expand the hive. They also bring back food and seek out new places to start a hive.

I laughed out loud. The little worker bees sound just like housewives. I wonder if one of the worker bees is called Donna Reed. They are really the lucky bees as they go flying around from flower to flower making delicious honey that feeds the hive, the queen, and the world. All the queen does is fertilize eggs. I'd much rather be a worker bee, wouldn't you? I wonder if the queen ever makes her own bed?

OOPS! MY SHADOW SIDE—WHAT WOLF DO I WANT TO FEED?

Prayer and Gratitude and Compassion

The first time I felt the vibrational power of love and gratitude flow through me was when I took a healing workshop led by Ron Roth, Ph.D. Dr. Roth had been a Roman Catholic priest for over twenty-five years when he left the church to become an international spiritual healer. His message is to open your heart to prayer as a healing process.

In his workshop, Dr. Roth told us his story and how we could heal ourselves and others. He said prayer is the key to tapping into healing energy. Like Reiki, as you pray, you tap into the Divine energy and become a conduit of the energy. I can feel the energy coming out of my hands when I place my hands on and around others. My hands get very hot, and I experience a current of energy flowing out. It's amazing! At the end of the workshop, the participants were asked to shut their eyes and be still. Then, Ron said, he and his partner would walk around the room and place their hand on our heads and not to worry. The song "Amazing Grace" started, and I shut my eyes tightly, waiting for my turn to feel the healing energy. I can only say there was a magical presence in the room, and when my head was touched, I felt so much gratitude and love overwhelming my body and soul I just sat there and cried. I couldn't speak.

There is no possible way I can describe this feeling; words are not enough. Gratitude and love flowed from my body. It was an energy of unexplained bliss and so powerful. It was here that I also learned when you speak from your heart to another person, their heart speaks back to you. Connecting with others through their hearts is powerful and so very loving. I enjoyed this feeling again many times when I was in the presence of Sai Maa. It feels like the presence of God's love. So powerful.

Ron Roth has since passed away, but he has written many books if you are interested in learning his message.

AARON'S COMMENTS ON GRATITUDE

On December 2, 1999, Aaron said, "Reflection is important. You need to reflect on what you have learned and what you are grateful for. All beings need to acknowledge what they have been given so that they will receive more. It's a payoff. The more gratitude, the bigger the next level of joy in your life. God needs to hear the feedback." He ended by saying, "Make prayers of gratitude in your life every day."

His Holiness, the 14th Dalai Lama, Teaches Compassion

I was overjoyed to see the Dalai Lama when he came to San Francisco years ago. Thousands of people attended this event, and most of the group sat quietly, waiting for him to appear. There was a hush in the crowd as the Dalai Lama entered and walked to the stage surrounded by his monks wearing their saffron robes. He sat there for a few minutes smiling at everyone. His eyes and smile reflected such love. I was in awe of him as he was so childlike and playful.

After a ceremony of lessons, chanting, and blessing, the Dalai Lama asked if anyone had a question. One man seated near the front of the stage stood up and asked, "How do you explain compassion?" The Dalai Lama sat still, scratching his head, and then said, "How I explain compassion. Go to any children's hospital and sit with the children for a while. You will feel compassion." I found that definition so powerful.

He was a representative of a loving, kind, and compassionate soul. At the end of the evening, everyone attending received a small blue Buddha, which I still have on my night table. It was an honor to be in his presence.

To wrap all the stories up, I want to share with you a story that had a significant influence in my awakening.

STORY OF A SOUL

I always start my classes reading this beautiful story, and I decided to end this book with it as well. I have enjoyed sharing some of my awakening stories. I understand I chose to come down as a spiritual being clothed as a human, and it has taken me a long time to finally put it all together.

The following is a story of the birth of a soul written by Dr. Tamar Frankiel and Rabbi/Cantor Judy Greenfield in their book, Minding the Temple of the Soul. This story always made me smile, and I loved telling it. The story is 'The Soul in the Body.'

'Story of a Soul'

"Soul," said God, "I have a mission for you."

A mission? The Soul thought only angels had missions. "Yes, I'm Ready," the Soul said aloud.

"You will go to earth for a certain period of time," God proclaimed.

"Earth? From what the angels say, it's dark and heavy there."

"Yes, compared to where you are. One of your jobs will be to bring light there."

"How do I do that?"

"You will receive instructions," said God. "There will be a time set aside for that."

"What is time?" the Soul asked.

God sighed. "It's very hard to explain, but when you're in it, you'll know it."

"Whatever you say," replied the Soul.

"You will also receive what you need to help you complete your mission," God continued. "It will also be hard to understand at first, but you'll have plenty of time to get used to it."

"You're talking about time again."

"All right. The point is, I am giving you something unique for your mission on earth. It is called a body."

"Thank you. But what is a body? No, I guess there's no point asking. I'll find out."

"That's right. Remember, the main thing is not to fear."

In a flash, the Soul found itself in a strange situation. It seemed to be in a kind of cave, smooth and soft all around. The energy was dense, but the Soul moved through it easily. At the same time, there was an embracing warmth, almost like being in the presence of the Creator.

Then an angel appeared, a presence of gentle light. The angel lit a candle and opened an immense book. The angel explained that the Soul was now inhabiting a body and would soon enter into the human world as a tiny member of the human species. The Soul listened and began to understand the wondrous purpose of existence, and the special role it would have in its earthly life. The angel also gave instructions, explaining how the Soul could stay connected with the spiritual world it had temporarily left behind. The knowledge was delicious—the Soul could even taste it. The Soul felt radiant with joy.

The angel gazed sweetly at the Soul, kissed it on its upper lip, just below the nose and, before the Soul could speak, disappeared. Warm darkness surrounded the Soul, and it slipped into a deep, restful sleep.

When it awoke, the Soul realized its body was going through a great change. There was pressure and movement. The Soul wondered what was happening and tried to remember what the angel had said. There was something about being on a mission—but what were the instructions the angel had given? The Soul suddenly realized its clarity of understanding was gone.

Panic rose, and the Soul wanted to escape. "Remember, the main thing is not to fear," an inner voice said.

The Soul quieted itself. But the urge to get out was strong. As the thoughts of escape grew louder, the Soul suddenly found itself being pushed with mighty force into what seemed to be a tunnel. In a moment, it was sliding down a canal toward a glimmer of light that reminded the Soul ever so slightly of home.

What a lift that small bit of light gave the Soul! Then a breeze swept through, a delicious breath of life, followed by a vibration, a sound that came from its own body. A moment later, the body was completely embraced, held, and rocked with a gentle motion. The Soul could focus now, and saw faces and eyes, almost as sweet as the angels. Voices, one low and one high, spoke nearby, and the happy words were like music. Those loving voices also reminded the Soul of the warmth and love of the Soul World. The Soul felt a great delight.

The surrounding energy began to settle into a calmer, more regular movement. Warmth now flowed into the body, a sweet-tasting liquid. Lips and fingers moved on soft, warm skin. The fragrances of body milk and fabric were a kaleidoscope, changing each moment.

The Soul was thrilled at this new beginning for its life. It poured its light into all these sensations, longing to express its surprise and happiness. Its eyes opened and sent a loving look to the eyes that gazed back with a smile.

The Soul knew a great miracle had occurred and sent a thankful song back to...whomever had brought it to this experience.

The Soul realized that the past, and all the places it had been, had become very hazy now. The Soul hoped it would find a way to remember.

> ***The greatest privilege of a human life is to become a midwife to the awakening of the Soul in another person.***
>
> **~ Plato**

The stories I've shared in this book are about how my soul entered its journey of remembering. I am delighted that you and your soul chose to explore through my adventures and hopefully, my experience will help others expand their journeys. My stories are have been my catalyst for personal growth. Through these stories, I hope you will find your journey to enlightenment as a midwife for your soul.

My wish for you is to connect with your guides, angels, and higher self. Once you ask for this wondrous connection, you will attract everything you'll need for any mission you are drawn to undertake in your life. The important part is paying attention, and once you do, you will begin to recognize all the signs and cues guiding you in the right direction. That is so fun! The universe hears you and assists you.

Synchronicities start once you are inside this state of flow. When this flow happens, you will not only know exactly what you need to accomplish your goals, you will know how to ask the universe for support. It is here where you begin to bring out the best in those around you by inspiring as well as guiding them. Pure potential and possibility are what you are, and pure potential and possibility is who everyone else is, too. Just as all things are possible for you, all things are possible for them, too.

The higher your consciousness, the more you elevate your thinking, the more you elevate your emotions, the more you elevate the way you feel, and the higher your vibration goes—you raise your vibration to raise your consciousness. You raise your consciousness to raise your vibration. The easiest way to raise your consciousness and raise your vibration is to do the things that bring you joy, inspiration, enthusiasm, excitement, and love.

I understand where you are. I know your potential and uniqueness. I have been there. In all the healing work I did on myself, I learned the journey of the unfolding process called my life had its own rhythm, and the way it was set up was perfect. I was told countless times the only way I could speed up my journey was through surrender. Leaving my controlling self behind was difficult for me, but when I finally asked for assistance, I watched miracles happen.

Once again, I repeat...

You alone are the master craftsman of your life. With the power of love, you become the master craftsman of the universe.

APPENDIX A: JOURNALING EXERCISE

These Journaling Exercises give you a new look into yourself. With new knowledge of old wounds, beliefs, and patterns, you can see with fresh eyes the book you have created. The question is, where do you go from here? In life, everything teaches you something. Every time you perform an act of kindness or move beyond yourself you create a new chapter in your book. Set your intention and begin. I promise you this life ride—your life!—is worth your every effort.

Now, close your eyes and take in that big, long inhale and exhale.

It's truly time to begin. What are you waiting for?

Use your journal to explore. Here are topics that require exploration:

What are my intentions?

Why do I think I was born?

What could be my unique gifts?

What am I yearning for?

What is my deepest desire?

Wounds

If we can see the patterns we are creating, we can change the patterns. This allows us to tell a new story.

Write down all of the wounds that pop up for you. Some of these wounds might include:

I am not enough.

I'm invisible.

I don't deserve.

I'm not wanted.

People always leave me.

I am not lovable and I don't matter.

I'm a failure.

I'm not important.

From the loving, adult person you are, ask yourself, "How old is this wound?" Witness your younger child with love and what he or she went through. The child didn't have the proper tools at the time. You can thank the child and offer a new way to look at what transpired.

> ***"It is harder to break a belief than to break an atom."***
>
> **~ Albert Einstein**

YOU CANNOT CHANGE A BELIEF UNTIL YOU DISCOVER WHAT IT IS

What are some of the beliefs you have about your life?

I'm not wanted.

People always leave me.

I am not lovable and I don't matter.

I'm a failure.

I'm not important.

I'm never going to be a success.

There is nobody out there for me.

I am too old, too young, too thin, too fat, and so on.

These old wounds (beliefs about your life) are shaping your experiences, and this is happening without you even realizing it. Fear of discovering these beliefs holds you back from a life you can create out of the old story.

CONNECTING WITH YOUR GUIDES, ANGELS, OR HIGHER SELVES

Communicating with your guides is not difficult. There's no magic formula. It doesn't matter if you feel you've done something wrong or if you don't go to your temple, church, or mass on a regular basis. All you must do is ask for their help. Guides and angels are not allowed to interfere in our lives unless they have been asked. There are many ways to communicate with your team (as I like to call them), from meditation, dreams, and writing in the shower to just listening. Once you ask your question, let your mind go blank and allow whatever comes forth. What comes to you may not make sense in the beginning but write down anything that takes your attention. As you review your journal, these thoughts and observations will all fall into place.

Acknowledgements

With all my love and gratitude for all the people who shared their gifts of time, editing, marketing and love assisting me on this journey of self-discovery.

Lynn Patner, M.S.W. *is a warm, funny, insightful and compassionate teacher. A Certified Hypnotherapist and Reiki Practitioner, Lynn's studies include Native American traditions, Shamanism, Eastern Traditions, a variety of energy therapies and healing practices. She weaves all of these disciplines into comprehensible teachings, providing tools to share with her clients and students. Lynn gives to those that wish to learn more, a sense of purpose and balance toward creating the life you have always desired, guiding them to experience the brilliance of their own inner light. Her mission in life is to assist others on the journey of awakening to their unlimited potentials and the uniqueness of their own being.*

As a social worker and children's advocate for San Mateo County Children and Family Services, Lynn's years of experience in working with individuals and families that are going through very difficult life transitions, has given her a deep level of compassion and respect for others and their individual life journeys. Her clear presence with others, in individual sessions and through workshops and seminars, comes forth in the knowing that every individual is unique, and carries within them a deep reservoir of wisdom.

Made in the USA
Columbia, SC
16 November 2021